Innovative Relevance

Innovative Relevance

Realigning the Organization for Profit

It is not a battle for the "shore lines"—
it's a struggle for purpose

Mark P. Dangelo

iUniverse, Inc.
New York Lincoln Shanghai

Innovative Relevance
Realigning the Organization for Profit

Copyright © 2005 by Mark P. Dangelo

iUniverse books may be ordered through booksellers or by contacting:

iUniverse
2021 Pine Lake Road, Suite 100
Lincoln, NE 68512
www.iuniverse.com
1-800-Authors (1-800-288-4677)

ISBN: 0-595-34246-9 (Pbk)
ISBN: 0-595-67081-4 (Cloth)

Printed in the United States of America

Dedicated in loving memory to Patrick

—a father should never outlive his children.

After all these years, your family has not forgotten.

TABLE OF CONTENTS

ACKNOWLEDGEMENTS

The writing of this book has taught me a great deal about people, publishing, family, and friends. Had it not been for the encouragement of a friend and editorial expert, Rick Grant, I would have never created this first book in the Innovative Relevance series. Rick has proven to be a valuable sounding board for ideas, content review, and publishing avenues. I owe him a great deal at a personal level, and he has my highest respect as a consummate professional and thought leader.

The creation of this book is based on over 20 years of working with some of the best professionals in the world. To these individuals, you have my thanks for the kindness and hospitality you have shown me over the decades.

Finally, to my wife Virginia who continually demonstrated her faith in my abilities. She endured many a night and dinner discussing and editing the content of the book during the creation cycle. My children, Nicole, and Jessica, who as they grow into responsible adults, will ensure my life is never dreary. And Patrick, whose death at an early age altered my destiny and outlook forever. Lastly, to my parents, as they had the foresight to push and guide me. Thank you.

FOREWORD

Each year, organizations throughout the industrialized nations spend billions of dollars on consultants, technology, and performance improvement initiatives with the hopes of gaining a strategic advantage, improving the bottom line, and anticipating an increase in share price. Unfortunately, a huge percentage of these initiatives fail to deliver on their promises, while distracting the organization from critical business issues. All too often, a decision or change in one area of the business directly or indirectly impacts several other areas.

Innovative Relevance is about how to address the complex array of challenges and constraints that impact virtually every organization, regardless of the size and industry. When an organization is facing a major initiative, restructuring itself, or responding to significant regulatory, competitive, and market issues, the ripple effect is felt by everyone—from the board to the receptionist, the customer, the supplier, and the stockholder.

Frequently, as the complexity and duration of an initiative increases, communications break-down, and a state of program entropy begins to set in. Individuals or groups start to focus less on the ultimate future state, and more on "going through the motions" of their individual assignments without regards to the critical linkages between program components. The program takes on characteristics of a death-march more than an adventure to a new way of doing business. As a result, staff turnover occurs, program costs skyrocket, schedules are missed, and valuable ROI opportunities are overlooked or lost.

These dramas are played out everyday in corporations across the globe in the form of strategic outsourcing, new technology initiatives, mergers, acquisitions, market adjustments, increased regulatory pressures, and new management agendas. Frequently, it seems that the larger or more established the organization gets, the greater the challenges become in dealing with change.

As the level of chaos and complexity in any initiative increases, we see that the ability of management to grasp and understand all the moving parts frequently decreases. Having worked through the intricacies of mergers, large systems deployments, new product launches, and other strategic initiatives as a manager, consultant, and vendor, there are many key "lessons learned" that can make life easier, if applied earlier in the process. *Innovative Relevance* could easily be described as "things we all learn along the way, but frequently forget to apply."

Among the most important of these lessons is the concept of *holistic or systems thinking*. In business, we are frequently bombarded with examples of success stories and case studies. Often these examples are one-dimensional and designed to push a specific agenda and in the process, mask bigger, more onerous problems (*e.g.,* WorldCom, Enron, Commerce One, and others.). Each of these aforementioned organizations were once touted as Wall Street "darlings" in their respective industries, but ended up costing shareholders billions of dollars in lost wealth.

Furthermore, as the number of variables in the initiative increases, the risk associated with a given program also escalates. The key to facing this challenge lies in recognizing and accepting the interrelationships of various constituents, processes, technologies, and constraints that impact success. It is these interrelationships or "touch points" that determine the degree of success or failure for many initiatives. Balancing the holistic "big picture," while dealing with the "devil in the details," is often one of the most important steps to ensuring victory in any endeavor.

Another important lesson learned is ability of teams to develop an effective and shared awareness of the "As-Is" state, the "To-Be" state, and the migration path. More often than we would like to admit, the road to success in great endeavors is laden with mixed messages, multiple versions of the truth, and conflicting agendas. Even if senior executives possess a clear view of the "future state," failure to get, and keep everyone on the same page is highly likely to result in catastrophe or disillusionment.

An all-to-common complaint of senior executives is that they are not getting the information they need, in a relevant context, to maximize their efficiency and effectiveness. Sarbanes-Oxley and other regulations have added a "personal touch" that demands closer attention to corporate accountability and transparency. The wide array of traditional applications found in any organization have resulted in formidable "silos of information" that require a team of business analysts to deal with a menu of technologies, with names like ETL, BI, EDW, and RDBMS to "connect the dots." Even after spending millions of dollars on IT, many decision-makers must still rely on fragmented reports that leave them "information impaired."

As we strive for the information that will help us better understand what is going on inside the organization and marketplace, the concept of relevance can be best summarized by Albert Einstein's quote—"Not everything that can be counted counts and not everything that counts can be counted." Thankfully, there is a new generation of specialized technologies emerging that package the power of applied analytics in modular, usable components. This aggregation of disciplines will allow executives to more easily see through the fog of data, and track what's important to their organization and shareholders regardless of where that information was generated.

Many business and leadership books promote trendy management solutions that are simply topical duct tape. *Innovative Relevance* delivers a structured framework that takes into consideration the numerous interrelated moving parts of today's enterprises, regardless of whether you are conducting a merger, acquisition, realignment, or business transformation. Created from proven experience, it is a comprehensive, holistic compilation of many of the lessons learned from a long journey through the trials and tribulations of many of America's largest, most visible corporations and consulting firms.

Michael Brooks

Introduction

THE FOUNDATION

It's not about the shorelines—a clear purpose is
required to realign the organization for sustained profits

Without relevance, many an approach or set of facts will suffice. We only have to look post-mortem at our countless improvement efforts that always seem to miss the mark. These include our investments made in machinery, ERP[i] processes and software, supply chains, customer relationship management (CRM), branding, market segmentation, or personnel. Our organizations look for successes and advantages onshore, offshore and, in fact, "anyshore." We try to keep pace with our competitors, blaze a new trail or restructure the enterprise for profitability, but our innovations are fraught with disillusionment, inferior economics, or a work force that fails to grasp its importance.

Yet as we listen to the headlines, sound bites, and management philosophy of the month, we are continually bombarded with the next innovation that promises to make us or our organization better. We struggle for change, success, and sustainability. Although foundationally, we persistently underestimate and misalign the resources, skills, and efforts needed. The changes based in the fundamentals of realignments and innovations have been lost, and as a result, so has our collective ability to sustain the initiatives.

Innovative relevance is not just about increases in productivity, loss of domestic jobs, cultural differences, cash flow, and most recently the certification of our financial statements. While each of these are important, the application of innovative relevance also includes the focused utilization of multiple disciplines that are seldom practiced today—ethics, integrity, passion, and consistency. The need for relevance lies within the people and the process—not just the technology.

While we all know that technology must support the innovative realignment, during the excitement of transition these efforts are overtaken by the movements happening in multiple departments, divisions, or geographic regions. These efforts can lose sight of their core principles and objectives all in a hurried attempt to show progress. The results are fragmented successes that cannot be leveraged across the enterprise.

Furthermore, in today's genre of politically correct communications, we've misplaced our ability to make and sustain these transformations without labeling everything we touch and see. Innovative Relevance is not a label; it's a realignment process for change that allows an organization to sustain those modifications, while taking advantage of new technological advancements. When I started in business over 20 years ago, the economics were for every one dollar spent on personnel, we spent three to four dollars on technology and supporting facilities[ii]. Today, those numbers are reversed and spreading further apart. People and processes are the keys for economic viability and productivity reformation.

Having spent the last 10 years working internationally with people of all races, cultures, and socio-economic statuses, the debate raging today within the G-7[iii] should not be about domestic workforces and protectionist measures. It should be about spending money for retraining, taking advantage of new in-demand skills, and continuous improvement of the workforce.

Historically, success has had a way of restricting innovation. We need to find the relevance in our new ideas, which comes not just from a novel design or modernization. Relevance comes from the application of innovation. Innovative relevance is most effective when used as part of a holistic and iterative approach for sustainable change, and the positive benefits that are included within the implications of its adoption.

Realignment is not a "one-off" endeavor that is meant to be practiced within a project team and then disbanded once 80% of the benefits have been achieved. It is a process that is meant to be included within other corporate improvement efforts such as Six Sigma, quality management, and business process management—as these key disciplines support a realignment and not vice versa. Critical executive and organizational initiatives of business intelligence, market research, branding, offshoring, and remediation are tools and strategies for transformation. They are not the end goal (discussed extensively in Chapter 6).

One last area that is continually talked about but often misunderstood is leadership. To establish an itinerary for realignment that is successful yet able to change with results and market conditions, a strong personal resolution and conviction of purpose is required. This is not to say blind faith or coercion will achieve your results. It is quite the contrary. Leadership in realignment efforts are about being bold, focused, passionate, humble and yes, flexible.

Realignment, from experience and continual practice, is very similar to farming in principles and results. It all starts with a conviction to achieve a product, but you need to start by preparing the soil and planting the seeds. This roadmap for the harvest does not happen overnight, but it does take careful planning and confidence to deal with events outside of your control (*e.g.,* weather, global gain prices, herd management, and lending practices). So as you begin your realignment process, you start as a "humble farmer" surveying your environment, planning for contingencies, and staying the course seeking profitable results. It is not a single endeavor or program that provides immediate gratification and it may not even be visible at the end of the quarter. It's a progression of iterative transformations and adjustments all meant to make sure you survive, while creating a longer-term purpose for sustainability.

This book is divided into four Sections with each one laying the foundation for restructuring success. The book is filled with learning diagrams to assist the reader with assimilation. Since most of us become skilled by reviewing materials and seldom read a book cover-to-cover, these illustrative diagrams will assist you with the rapid examination and personal internalization of the realignment concepts. Additionally, the appendices provide you a cornerstone of baselining assessment questions and techniques, necessary to properly plan for the innovative relevance actions required to profitability complete the realignment programs.

SECTION 1

THE BASICS OF ALIGNMENT

"I start where the last man left off"
—Thomas A. Edison

Aligning any organization begins with a realization for change coupled with an integration of definitive requirements. Frequently, realignment efforts begin with an outsourcing or a cost containment initiative. While these are worthy goals, they are not sufficient standalone rationale for realignment programs. These initiatives can be easily misguided and fail to meet the requirements of the organization due to changing economic, market, or political necessities.

The next four chapters articulate the success criteria and disciplines that you and the organization must master as part of an innovative relevance realignment initiative. Too often, we rely only on our historical experiences or those gleaned from textbooks or classroom settings. As we all know, leadership is not management. Realignment is not about developing a business plan. Innovative relevance is not about a turnkey solution or application. Innovative relevance starts with a purpose, supported by direction, experience, integrity, and leadership.

Chapter 1: It Starts with Vision and Principles

Chapter 2: Motivation, Ethics, and Integrity

Chapter 3: Experience Counts

Chapter 4: Engage the Extended Organization

Chapter 1

It Starts with Vision and Principles
Define the rationale for success

Technology is everywhere we turn. It is appearing in nearly every facet of our existence. Unprecedented technology adoption is irrevocably changing the way we conduct business, interact with each other, and the way we live. In today's multinational commerce environments, at the first sign of a problem our immediate reaction for a solution is the deployment of technology and most recently outsourcing. Yet, is the utilization of technology or the invocation of an outsourcer really the answer? If we offload a troubled division or department to a low cost provider or implement an updated ERP version, will this address our reoccurring quarterly performance problems? What new challenges will it create? Are we using the "philosophies of the day" on business processes which are already not "efficient," only to find that with the adoption of a new solution the inefficiency is achieved faster and now resides in a new "opportunity?"

We keep seeking a panacea, a silver bullet, which will launch our company and ourselves into the forefront of our industry. Many a business manager looks for a solution that will provide employees with tremendous productivity gains and intellectual knowledge, while minimizing costs and improving corporate market share. We are conditioned by vendors to think that technology products hold the solution to our problems. Outsourcers are quietly telling domestic customers that they are better, faster, and cheaper than local workforces. Just turn on the television set, open a trade journal, read a newspaper, or log onto the Internet. We are shown many "success" stories of companies who have gained business or competitive advantages by using these approaches. Since they accomplished this feat, should we not be able to use the same approach and technologies to get the similar if not better results? These solutions are ubiquitous and interchangeable so why wouldn't they work for us? We are just as dedicated and skilled as our competitors, right?

This technological evolution and the search for instantaneous results are indeed thought provoking with the potential for extraordinary returns. We are living in a time of unprecedented change and turmoil and there appears to be no end in sight. Nonetheless, the deployment of non-core solutions never seems to materialize as quickly as expected or with the results anticipated. This disparity is caused by a lack of comprehension for the organization's business drivers and how they can affect quality, productivity, or costs. Until these inter-relationships are understood, we will always fall short of the desired organizational and personal measurements. We need an unambiguous vision for sustained transformation and realignment, and we need to be passionate about their achievement. We start to define our vision for realignment by understanding our own basis for decision making and leadership.

Recognize your principles

Sometimes to project forward, we must look back and understand the premises of our success. As leaders and managers, we have inherently established our success on clear principles. These principles are supported by[iv]:

- **Rationale**—why are the principles important?
- **Implications**—what are the consequences of adopting these principles?

Numerous individuals will espouse principles, but they lack the required internalization needed to make them successful. The communication of their principles is simply words—not beliefs that can guide a sustainable realignment effort. Without all-inclusive rationale and implications for internalization, principles of realignment breakdown creating strife and conflict during the realignment efforts.

The formulation of principles sounds simple. Yet each and every word requires careful reflection and unhurriedness. A principle starts with an unequivocal statement. It is not a generic statement. It is not the shared values of your organization. This is about your beliefs and value system, and how it can create a correct realignment vision.

A useful technique for identifying and refining your principles can be seen in *Figure 1.1*.

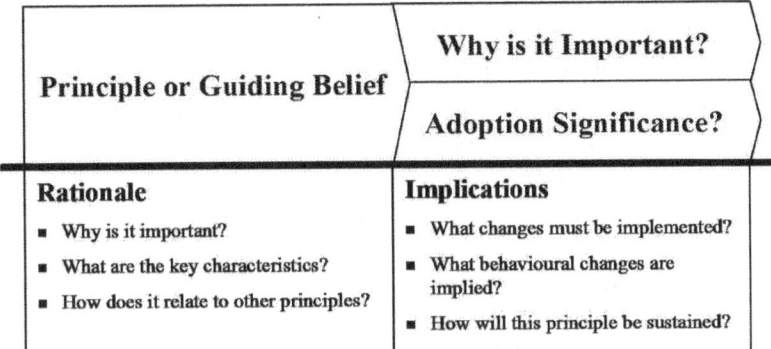

Principle or Guiding Belief	Why is it Important?
	Adoption Significance?

Rationale	Implications
■ Why is it important?	■ What changes must be implemented?
■ What are the key characteristics?	■ What behavioural changes are implied?
■ How does it relate to other principles?	■ How will this principle be sustained?

Figure 1.1—Principles ("So What? Who Cares?")

A rule of thumb to determine if you have the appropriate refinement and intent is to have no more than 10 guiding principles and no fewer than 6.

Examples of comprehensive principle statements include:

- Focused job training and educational activities will be sought that create a personal work and learning environment, which facilitate increases in the quality and effectiveness of my daily actions.

- Leadership will be demonstrated by adherence to the highest moral codes of conduct and ethics ensuring that accountability is inherent in all communications, work efforts, and actions.

- Experience will be gleaned from all work activities building upon prior successes, while recognizing and seeking out those behaviors that promote continual personal expansion.

While these statements may not reflect your personal principles, they clearly demonstrate the specificity required to sufficiently articulate the important rationale and implications needed for team building and consistency of purpose.

What are the realignment principles?

You may ask why we started with the articulation of your personal principles rather than launch headfirst into the realignment process? The answer lies with experience. To be an effective and successful realignment leader, you have to believe in the goals of the effort and they have to align closely with your personal foundation. Unlike the reality shows and music of today, it is very hard to fake the commitment needed for alignment if you are diametrically opposed to the principles needed for its success. An opposing dichotomy can create dysfunctionality between you and your transition team. If left unchecked, this polarization of principles will soon reduce the pace of change to a crawl and in some cases, result in financial ruin.

Now, with the insight of your challenge (*i.e.*, to realign the organization using innovative relevance) and your own internal principles defined and focused, what are the principles and corresponding vision for the effort you have been selected to perform?

For our usage, the vision is the end goal or desired "steady state." Like the farmer we introduced earlier, you find yourself at the start of the growing season. The snow has melted, the outlook for grains is moderate, and the need for livestock (*e.g.*, cows, pigs, sheep, chicken) have increased 15% thanks to the recent diet fads. Your goal is to maximize profits using your 452 acres of land, three barns, two John Deere tractors, and two hired hands. Your vision to achieve this resides with a suitable mix of crop farming, pasture management, equipment maintenance, cash flow (for seeds, fertilizer, payroll, and sprays), and the ever unpredictable and unforgiving Mother Nature.

In our corporate world, like the farmer, we may have numerous interim goals to arrive at the end-state. However, we need to plainly understand the desired outcome, and how it will be supported with the resources and plans necessary to achieve it. Our vision is also reinforced by the principles of realignment that are the foundation for not only achieving the interim goals supporting the vision, but also for the decision making that is required every day. An example of these relationships is seen in *Figure 1.2*.

Consequently, for an organization to get the correct results, it must understand the business requirements that direct the vision and organizational realignment principles. You, as the leader of ensuring the innovative relevance of decision and implementation actions, must be able to deploy solutions that meet the needs and expectations within the identified organizational constraints (*e.g.*, costs, resources, priorities).

Nevertheless, it has become apparent from the numerous industry studies and post implementation reviews that as decision makers, we have misplaced our ability to understand that the solutions (either operational, personnel, or technology) are enablers; not the primary drivers. Relevant innovations provide us with "transformation tools" for the realignment from an "As-Is" state to a "To-Be" state of improvement. Innovative relevance provides the filter for the effective determination of accurate change mechanisms or solutions. It assists organizations and people with the transition from the current unproductive present state to a superior, well-organized, and effective projected state using a foundation of principles to guide the efforts. Innovations and technologies are not the panacea of the management folklore that we are exposed to on a daily basis. It's seldom a turn-key approach and whether it is done internally or via external outsourcers, the results will be the same.

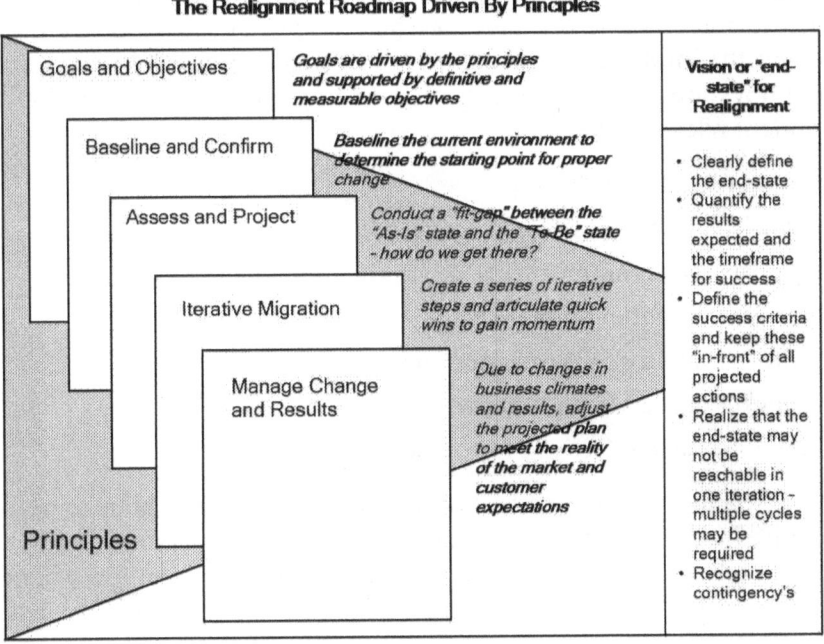

Figure 1.2—The Principle Foundation

So what? Who cares?

To be a realignment leader in an organization, an individual must possess an integrated and comprehensive vision for the projected or "To-Be" environment. It is well known that there are always organizational participants that believe any modification will lead to failure or a lack of effectiveness. As a result, the ability to influence people and processes, at times, is an uphill struggle. Yet, this struggle is precisely why an instantly recognizable vision coupled with an integrated set of principles for realignment is needed to ensure that the innovative relevance programs are achieved. Without a set of defensible and methodical "meta-data" driven criteria, we cannot hope that the organization will understand our actions, internalize them, and help us achieve success.

Failure to grasp the importance of this chapter will condemn your endeavor before you start. As realignment leaders and change agents, we are required to provide guidance and fervor, which are necessary for sustained and continued improvements during the transition efforts.

Additionally, personal convictions coupled with a well-defined realignment vision are key success factors in program goal and objective realization. As a leader, you must be the one who not only understands the program's relevance, but the implications and value of implementing or deferring the projected innovations. Critical benefits of providing this passion and vision for a realignment relevance are:

- organizational leadership,
- consistency of technology directions,
- management commitment,
- empowerment of employees,
- informed and quality decision making,
- quicker delivery with minimal resistance, and
- an increase in effective communication.

Without a fitting vision and set of principles, you cannot hope to promote the required transfer of knowledge needed for success. Moreover, your ability to extract and leverage the individual skills from each team member will not be accomplished without in-depth communications surrounding the realignment's purpose and end-state. The dissemination of the vision, strategy, and direction must be consistent and continual to the organizations (internal and external), customers, investors, board members, and critical alliance partners.

For the realignment to be successful and sustaining, a leader must be able to articulate the vision and goals of the process to the team members. The team members become extensions of the leader and their commitment to the migration efforts. The team must be allowed to:

- question the vision,
- assimilate the vision in their words,
- challenge the process to improve its acceptance, and
- make changes as a "cooperative" or high-performance team.

The team members are the front line speakers and advocates for transformation within the organization. They can positively influence the organizational personnel in a non-threatening manner, even if the leader is viewed with suspicion.

The realignment leaders must conduct themselves in a manner that is consistent with the communicated vision and migration plans. A fundamental reason for program "failure" is leaders and teams that can speak to the vision and directions, but lack the will and ability to execute the appropriate changes. From experience, this inability to "Walk the Talk" contributes between 30% and 60% of the realignment disillusionments, failures, and stoppages. The best conceived and articulated plans are ineffective without the leaders and teams adhering to their own principles, directions, standards, and plans. Consistency and repeatability will be key requirements for leaders to transform the organizational culture, while having personnel assimilate the foundational premises of the realignment.

Lessons learned

Innovative relevance is not driven by technology or globalization. It is driven by a defined, communicated, and validated vision supported by properly aligned principles of operation. Only with the appropriate allocation of technology and globalization against a validated set of goals and objectives, can an organization derive sustainable profits.

Since personnel are majority contributors to all realignment programs, the definition and communication of the realignment rationale and implications will provide commonality of purpose for employees, consultants, and subject matter experts (SME's).

- Vision must be supported by business drivers and personal convictions.

- Principles are not generic; they must provide meaningful and sustainable directions for the stated vision.

- Goals and objectives are required to obtain the necessary measurements and milestones needed for iterative migration programs (detailed explanation in Chapter 7).

- Realignment efforts are not "one-offs" and are seldom achievable with one set of programs or single series of events.

- Passion, while critical to motivation, is not a substitute for vision and principle articulation and validation.

- The ability to influence and sustain commitment of the organization starts with a validated vision.

- Listen, communicate, and educate.

Chapter 2

Motivation, Ethics, and Integrity
Accountability rests with the realignment personnel

Unless you're reading a book on ethics and integrity, you will usually find this chapter at the end of the book. It's a topic much talked about—but seldom seen and little practiced. Yet, when we examine the breakdown in organizational leadership globally, we clearly see a need for truth, honesty, and conviction in action. In today's global business climates, it appears we have reached a state of legislating common sense and ethical conduct to ensure corporate officers adhere to generally accepted business practices. Today, there are over 15,000 federal, state, and local laws[v] governing ethical conduct, corporate reporting, and financial management to protect the environment, the economy, investors, employees, and creditors. Furthermore, employee productivity has leveled off with personnel expressing the highest degree of dissatisfaction with their employers in nearly 15 years.

In 2004, we saw a bold move by CitiGroup's chief executive officer attempting to realign the largest financial services institution in the world. We witnessed the CEO fire three of his senior executives as part of an effort to demonstrate the need within the conglomerate for higher ethical conduct and personal integrity. It clearly demonstrated the brand's overarching conviction and bold passion leading a multicultural and global workforce. However in 2005, we are shocked yet again with additional indignities in the insurance and life-sciences industries. These actions continually devastate the stock market and investor confidence, while incurring the wrath of customers and prosecutors.

The reality of our professional condition

Take a look around and you can see and feel the newfound distrust, negativity, and general contempt being projected to anyone with a management or leadership role. Motivation and teamwork has been the foundation for productivity increases experienced over the last 10 years. Yet over the last 18 months, growth has stagnated, world markets have slumped, and people have become less tolerant and understanding of change within the organizational hierarchy. The motto of the current corporate employee is "tell me another one." The relentless downsizing, resizing, restructuring, and corporate indictments, have created a workforce that is lacking the commitment, passion, and energy needed for successful transformation and sustained delivery. Outside the corporate offices the current motivation is simple—survival.

Employers and managers have instituted "town hall" meetings, weekend retreats, and "breakfast for the staff" all in an effort to motivate personnel to achieve a common agenda. On the other hand, it's hard to work together when you're competing for job security against your peers. In essence, a by-product of the constant downsizing has created a "win-lose" situation within the teams, as competition has produced dysfunctionality and substandard results. Additionally, ethics are also being strained as professionals unaccustomed to job insecurity are seeking any means necessary to secure the hierarchy of needs basic to human survival and psyche[vi]. An employee of a services company who provided five years of dedicated service summarized, "…it looks like my boss is going to lay off more personnel so he can get a bigger bonus to meet his goals. Since I'm the only FTE (fulltime equivalent) left in this functional position (the rest are temps), it doesn't take a genius to figure out I'm next." You can imagine the feeling of ill will and hopelessness that permeates the culture of this organization in realignment. She was laid off three weeks later.

Five motivational tenets

So within the current uncertain economic and employment environment, how can you hope to influence personnel behavior, while at the same time improving the bottom line using innovative relevance? Over the last two decades, I have found five fundamental tenets (see *Figure 2.1*) that continue to deliver positive results with staff during realignment activities. Additional principles can be added within given situations, but these five consistently provide the best results for all levels of personnel.

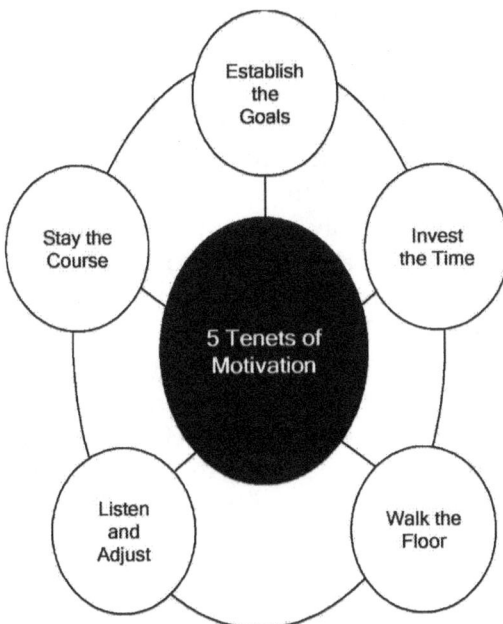

Figure 2.1—Motivational Tenets

1. **Establish the Goals:** The foundation of a motivated team is a common set of goals (with subordinate measurable objectives). The goals should contain short-term (less than 90 day) and long-term (over 12 month) goals that are realistic and achievable. The goals must stretch the employees without breaking their spirit or being too difficult to achieve. Furthermore, the needed training and educational goals, which are dependencies of achieving profitability, efficiency, and marketing objectives, should be included within the overall plan. The culmination of these goals is a cohesive and focused agenda that sets the motivational foundation. The strategies you select for achievement must also be delineated or your agenda will be relegated to collecting dust on a shelf.

2. **Invest the Time:** Once you've got an initial agenda, it's now time to communicate its purpose and your personal intent to the staff. This is not a one-time activity. It is not a unilateral communiqué. It is a monthly or quarterly activity that spends only one-half of the time communicating directions. The remainder of the time is spent listening and clarifying directions and commitments. Constant communication is critical as the corporate "grapevine" can twist the key deliverables and measures that you're seeking within your plan. Also, political and economic changes will effect the directions you establish.

These challenges require additional communications throughout the life of the realignment efforts. Organizational excellence starts with you.

3. "**Walk the Floor**": Get out of your office. It is amazing not only the "goodwill" that can be established, but also the information that can be learned. Failure to get involved with your employees and peers can result in a "window dressing" appearance to motivation. When you're not traveling, personally walk the floors, at least once daily and at different times, to ensure that you meet everyone over a period of a week. When traveling to a remote office, keep this behavior to ensure consistency among all employees regardless of location. This is a hard lesson to learn. Remember, positive and negative feelings about you and your directions from employees (regardless of their time zones or continents) travel back to the home office even before you return. If you fail to act consistently, then you will fail to positively influence staff and results.

4. **Listen and Adjust:** You cannot hope to achieve the best possible results without feedback from staff, coupled with a good measurement program. The staff needs to embrace the program goals and to internalize them. People embrace transformations when they can get involved and have a voice in their own destiny. We cannot dogmatically assume that our direction must be followed explicitly and without deviation. Even strong disciplines like Six Sigma inherently have diversity and variability within their foundation. Failure to allow for their input will stifle creativity and doom the long-term benefits of any program. Reward those employees who demonstrate positive attitudes and achieve results consistent with the agenda.

5. **Stay the Course:** Don't forget, when you get out in front of an issue or the organization, you can also become the target of politics and skeptics. In fact, even some of the employees that you're seeking to motivate can become an issue with others in the team. Deal with dissenting team members privately, but quickly. Establish a format for acceptable behavior in these cases and continue to review it at least weekly with the employee. You will also be compelled to defend your staff within the corporate arena. Failure to support the team in their actions of delivering the goals within the agenda will create rapid motivational deterioration.

Bottom line, motivating a team or a division is hard work and not straightforward. It requires more time and energy on your behalf especially during these uncertain periods. It is not just about process. It is not about methods or tools. It is about the people. People who are committed and motivated to results are the underpinning of your success. To motivate these people requires a leader who has integrity, ethics, purpose, and focus. Employees need and want a leader who speaks the truth, while leaving the politics to the politicians.

Motivation. Commitment. Passion. All of them intangible. All of them critical. Without suitable motivation, without your staff behind your directions, without a passionate commitment towards results, it's time to surrender. Without these critical success factors, it is time to seek another profession and new job openings in the Sunday classifieds.

Add our ethical and integrity challenges

For the last 40 years, we have challenged our employees and peers on accepting the disciplines of loyalty, hard work, company values, and corporate ethics. However, few industries have been spared the drastic reversal of fortunes that corporate personnel have felt personally and professionally in the last three years. In many cases, the need for profits and budget controls has demoralized the organization, as it has become every person for themselves—"to Hell with the corporate agenda."

Yet, as professionals and corporate officers, we do have a responsibility to deal with all personnel, vendors, and clients with respect and honesty. If we act with less than exemplary behavior, we propagate an image deserving of the typically thankless treatment, which so often is leveled at the hard working operators, technicians, administrators, and managers.

How can you make certain that employees and contractors working on a demanding realignment effort behave with the most exemplary conduct possible (see *Figure 2.2*)?

Figure 2.2—"The Circle of Ethics and Integrity"

Lead by Example: Set the tolerance limits on behavior and tackle tough situations head-on. Failure to address difficult issues creates a perceived lack of integrity and decision-making ability about you and your organization.

Communicate your Values: What is important to you and your team? Are they aware of the consequences and implications of violating or voiding your directives and professional criteria? Failure to communicate can create a vacuum for inappropriateness.

Be Decisive and Consistent: The inability to decide on a difficult issue will generate an atmosphere of acceptance for aberrant behavior. Failure to act consistently from issue to issue will result in confusion and rejection of the model you're attempting to envisage.

Be Honest and Clear: Too often personnel fail to communicate all the details and implications of events in straightforward language. Trying to cover up a self-inflicted event using arcane "management speak" will create far worse consequences than the event ever could. The ability to positively influence people and processes will be superiorly served with open dialogues and truthfulness.

Challenge Others to Perform: An island is a lonely place to be when you're stranded without companionship and assistance. Network with other divisions and groups on the codes of conducts you and the team embraces. Track the progress and establish qualitative and quantitative measures that can be reported in the "dashboard."

Manage Perceptions: Corporate image is critical to ensuring that ethical behavior is rewarded and encouraged. Frequently, personnel feel that senior management lacks an appreciation for their complex work and long-hours of constant retraining. Senior personnel must be informed, and understand the agenda and action that you are employing for consistent ethical behavior.

Listen to Others: An excellent way to continually enhance ethical standards is to listen to others. Outside influences can augment conduct rules and acceptance from staff and peers. It also provides a continual transformation mechanism for on-going improvements.

Remember, business lives and perishes by the daily operations contained within the extended company environments (see Chapter 14). We are the caretakers of this critical business environment. If we permit our peers and employees to behave with less than the highest standards of conduct, then we will create a self-fulfilling prophesy for failure.

Examples of ethical conduct and leadership integrity

Observance of corporate ethics requires the manager to maintain a constant vigil while adhering to uncompromising principles. Nevertheless, the adherence to uncompromising ethical beliefs is seldom clear-cut within real world events. This ambiguity is created by the impact of disciplining personnel or reversing a decision made weeks before. This reversal can potentially have serious operational consequences on personnel and results. Let's examine a couple of real-life ethical situations[vii] and the impact the decisions had within the operational environments.

Case 1: Dealing with critical shift personnel

The Situation: Joe was an excellent technical services manager. He possessed 20 years of solid and progressive experience, and with the recent hiring of a new CIO[viii], he found himself with newfound responsibilities and commitments including an offshore data center. Joe was extremely well respected by his peers and his staff.

The Event: One night during the production schedule, Sally the lead third shift operator, called Joe to notify him that numerous abends[ix] were creating a critical situation that would significantly impact the online SLA[x]'s for the coming day. She informed him that they followed procedure to the letter and that some unknown and unplanned event must have created this "new situation." Joe immediately called a "Severity 1" situation and all resources were mobilized to address the recovery and to ensure SLA's would not be impacted. It didn't work.

The Result: Upon a "post-review" of the events, it was uncovered that this was not the first time this situation had occurred (as it was created by operators not following procedure coupled with inferior training). Furthermore, it was discovered that Sally was not even available for much of the evening to her shift personnel as she was busy "studying for an exam." This also was not a first-time event. Joe had uncovered the facts, but when asked by the CIO for the full-account, Joe did not disclose the damaging situation created by Sally. Joe knew that all this could have been prevented, but he also did not want to lose Sally as a result of her being disciplined for lack of leadership and judgment. After all, when she applied herself she was an excellent resource and a good manager. Who else could Joe get to cover 3rd shift?

The staff began to adopt poor habits as a result of Sally's continual "absence" from the shift. The 3rd shift staff also knew that the consequences of inferior performance were neither positive nor negative, as no action was taken by Joe to correct the situation now or in the past. When the CIO learned of the correct events from a financial analyst (word travels fast when it's "bad"), Joe's unethical communication, indecisiveness, and not holding his employees to the highest standards, created an unworkable situation between himself and the CIO. Sally left two months later followed by Joe.

Ethical Lessons Learned: Honesty in communication coupled with decisive action could have prevented this event and saved their careers. Joe's failure to lead his groups by a strong example of integrity and accountability resulted in staff performance that was sub-par. He wanted to avoid confrontation, but in the end, he found his negative ethical behavior was far worse than his interpersonal fears. Failure to act and communicate consequences to staff contributed to the outsourcing of all technical services functions to a large service provider. The culture of delivery could not be changed to meet the CIO's agenda established by the new senior management team. In the end, everyone suffered from Joe's behavior.

Case 2: Using new techniques to hide inappropriate behavior

The Situation: A COO[xi] of a technology firm was seeking effective methods to improve service delivery within her teams, while at the same time improving efficiency and individual productivity. She reviewed many improvements and process techniques, but determined that the well-publicized Six Sigma approach would be the one selected for her organizational environments. It was eventually adopted as a corporate standard and applied enterprise wide.

The Event: Several studies were launched; help desk, operations, and network support. While these were not the only ones within IT, they were the most visible by her as she felt they were not customer focused and were significantly overstaffed. The teams were staffed properly and trained with the necessary knowledge to complete their Six Sigma missions. However, when the teams presented their findings and improvement efforts, the COO dismissed their results as flawed and ill-conceived. The black belts on these engagements were dumbfounded, and could not understand the rationale behind the rejection of efforts to improve efficiency and customer satisfaction that met the stated goals of the efforts. The COO made a unilateral decision on the improvement actions that would be taken, and publicly declared them successes of the new corporate wide strategy. There was neither discussion nor debate on this matter with the teams.

The Result: Even though the teams were demoralized with the actions dictated by the COO, they were implemented per her instructions—a 20% across the board reduction in personnel effective immediately. The customers began to experience decreased service levels, longer wait times in queues, and network disruptions. The personnel began to suffer under extreme work hours, increased stress, higher turnover, poor communication, and a hostile work environment. A month after the actions were implemented, the CEO was at a dinner event with an external customer who used the services of this corporation. The customer cornered the CEO to express displeasure with his organization's lack of commitment to excellence (due to inferior services being delivered to the customer).

Having been caught completely unaware, the CEO quickly learned that the real focus of the new initiative instituted by the COO was not driven by the "customer or quality"—only by cost savings. The program was neither in line with his directives nor the spirit of his continuous improvement and quality vision. The COO explained that the actions were indeed a "by-product" of the team's excellent work and she was taking the next logical step to improve efficiency. After all, she came from the IT ranks and her actions were completely justified based upon her experiences. She neglected to explain the team's viewpoint, their detailed, process-based decisions, and the fact that she gave them the decision and told them to make the data fit. The CEO eventually found out the truth of the situation and the events that failed to recognize the "voice of the customer."

The team's initial recommendations were again reviewed and this time the new champion of these efforts subsequently adopted them. The customer satisfaction eventually rose but their market reputation had been significantly damaged. The delivery personnel felt betrayed by management once again and the rift exists still today. The COO's deception to her boss not only affected her career, but nearly 25% of the remaining staff resigned to pursue new opportunities outside of the corporation for a total turnover rate of 45% within a nine month period.

Ethical Lessons Learned: Many ask in this situation, what the COO did wrong, as this type of situation presents itself frequently across many industries. The fact is we have become immune to people deceiving staff and higher ups. It has become part of the generic "corporate fabric" that we deem acceptable (after Enron, the above event seems hardly noteworthy). The ends justify the means, right? Wrong. Leadership and ethical behavior starts with you and your staff.

When we fail to challenge others to uphold accurate communication, honesty, strong values, and respect for staff, we condone a culture of liars, cheaters, and deceivers. The COO's inability to listen to others created an unworkable situation. She lacked ethical behavior towards the staff, team and her own manager. In spite of this, she still holds her current title albeit with reduced responsibilities.

Case 3: Courageous leadership—successful communication

The Situation: Joan, the Manager of Operations, was recently hired to instill strong process and discipline to a staff of 300 across 15 different time zones. Logistics alone created serious communication difficulties, but due to the rapid nature of the core business, expansion plans would create an even larger group within the next 15 months. It had been brought to Joan's attention by Human Resources that some personnel in her departments had been previously terminated for significant offenses, which included sexual harassment, drugs, language, insubordination, "ditching" work, falsified time and expense reports, and the list went on.

The Event: Joan needed to begin a program that announced her operating values to the staff which was diverse and multi-cultural. The staff also had communication and dialect issues that resulted in miscues effecting SLA's. She spent the first 30 days understanding the composition of her team members, while working with human resources to develop an agenda that would convey her principles, acceptable behaviors, and teamwork guidelines (in addition to definitive corporate policies). While the effort would have consistent core elements, it would be changed slightly to ensure that key messages were delivered to selected groups who needed specific attention in given areas.

The Result: Joan implemented a multi-pronged approach. She went to each location conducting "town hall" sessions. During these sessions, which every employee was required to attend, she outlined her plan of action for the groups. The sessions were interactive where employees were given a chance to challenge her values and directions, while at the same time clarifying her intentions. As part of this clarification process, the employees could internalize the values and ethical guidelines. She addressed the prior issues within the groups while providing decisive and consistent guidelines for behavior and conduct.

Employees, while initially skeptical, watched over a period of 12 months her reinforce the statements and directions made during these initial sessions. That's right, she repeated at least every quarter, the town hall session for the complete group. She conducted these in person, via conference call, video conferencing or some times several at once for multiple simultaneous locations. As time progressed, the employees realized that "she was who she said she was." During her first year, the number and severity of ethical violations decreased by over 80%. Even during a recent set of separations to trim down an over staffed department within her group, she received an outstanding rating from the departing employees.

Ethical Lessons Learned: The correct way to establish ethical conduct within your department, team or group is to be courageous and "get out in front" of the issues. If the employees don't know your guiding values and ethical principles, then you are putting them immediately at a disadvantage. You must lead by example even when the path is difficult and unpopular. Consistency is also a key success factor as you manage the expectations of staff and your senior management. If you act with the highest ethical standards, employee morale and results will improve significantly. Without proper conduct, you will never be able to challenge others to perform at the highest conduct possible.

Lessons learned

When team or leadership integrity fails, the organization will condemn the realignment efforts to the same fate. Adherence to a stringent and publicized set of ethical standards for all realignment efforts is mandatory. Motivational consistency rests on a foundation of integrity and ethical behavior.

- Realignment programs and efforts must use an articulated set of acceptable behaviors.
- Integrity of the programs team can never be a subject of debate or question.
- Motivation must be a key managerial skill for all team leaders, due to the uncertainty generated within realignment programs.
- Accountability for behavior must be maintained; aberrations must be quickly addressed and corrected (see Chapter 15).
- Realignment programs will face reviews, audits, and scrutiny.
- Ethical compromises are the grounds for team removal (see Chapters 9 and 15).
- Failures in integrity and ethical behavior are not recoverable and rarely mitigated.

Chapter 3

Experience Counts
Achieving relevance using proven knowledge

In its undeveloped form, experience is greatly influenced by numerous character traits, work ethics, intelligence, and personal ambitions. Each time we seek a new employee or business partner, we are looking for specific characteristics and capabilities that we believe will help meet or exceed organizational goals. These traits represent a sequence or set of qualifications that we do not possess as either an individual or as an organization.

Just before I started writing this book, I was speaking with an accomplished executive recruiter regarding branding, skills, and experiences needed, to compete in the markets of the future where innovative relevance will play a material part in organizational profitability. Our discussion concentrated on searches being conducted for management consulting clients, who were providing strategic and expert advice to various industry cross-segments. Much to my surprise, the critical criteria for client presentation was not experience, but the academic background and publication history of the candidates.

Since I was perplexed on the importance of this rationale, I continued to ask probing questions on the justification for this criterion. The recruiter put it even more succinctly for me, "Our present orders are for strategist and most firms actually run away when they see too much implementation in a resume." I hope I don't hire his consulting clients for any future work I am planning!

Contrary to the executive recruiter above, the application of innovative relevance for realignment efforts requires proven cross-domain experience that is significant and encompassing. Innovative relevance is not an exercise or a project that can be treated with as a "one-off" using vertical skills, academic research, and canned software applications. The model for required realignment experience is best demonstrated in *Figure 3.1*.

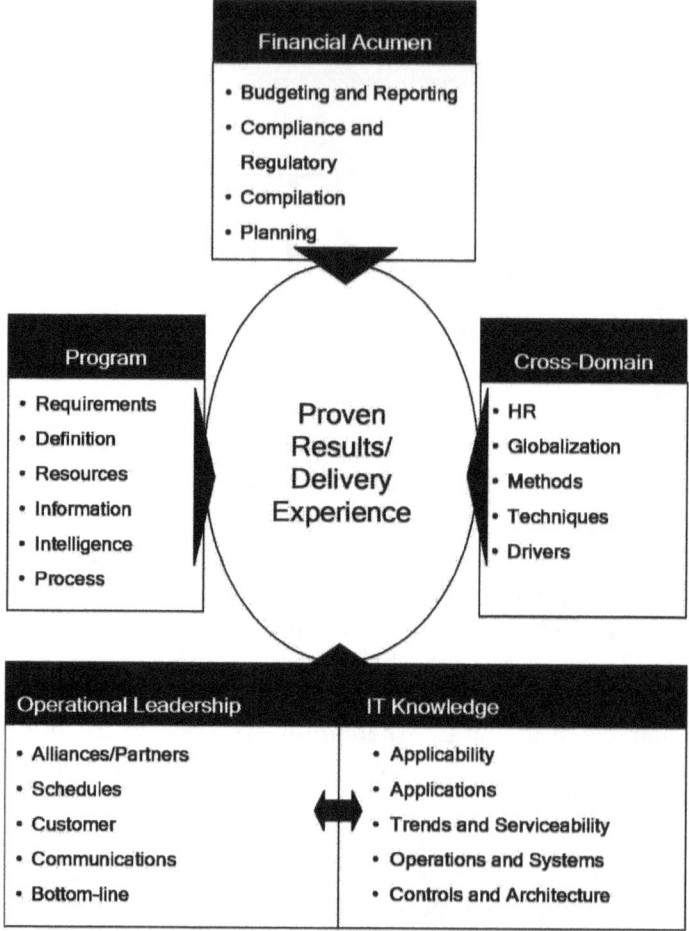

Figure 3.1—The Experiential Model for Innovative Relevance

The model above is one that works regardless of your specific industry. It works whether you're a public or private organization. It works regardless of your organizational culture or your profit objectives. It works if you're a startup, or a firm entering your 100th year of operations. From experience, it works.

Financial acumen

From today's headlines few places offer a more striking example of the pride of human hopes, than corporate executive offices. And nowhere does this seem truer than in how corporate leaders assess the return of investments and ongoing operational costs against bottom-line results.

Moreover, corporate boards and independent directors are tasked with evaluating the day-to-day value on a multitude of levels. Is the company getting superior returns from its investments in personnel? Is it providing adequate worth to its shareholders? What value, post-WorldCom, are the alliances and programs contributing towards bottom-line results? Too often, precise, quantifiable measurements are frequently deduced, inferred, or extrapolated using equal amounts of faith, hope, and sometimes wishful thinking.

Forget for a moment, if you can the potentially criminal behavior of Wall Street prognosticator's, consultant's (*e.g.*, audit, tax, and management) paper shredders, and certain corporate board members. In a best-case scenario, what they have represented is the full and total blindsiding of executives who, to a greater or lesser degree, subscribed to "the-greater-the-complexity-the-greater-the-value" axiom. Solid financial acumen and experience has been replaced with corporate spin and elaborate public relations.

Once a task relegated to "bean-counters" of the back office, stringent financial acumen has always been a critical skill and experience set for the realignment professional. Within the new millennium's delivery and approval cycles, we have witnessed a breakdown in very large and small corporations that have resulted in increased legal and political focus for the assurance of accurate financial accounting and reporting (see *Figure 3.2*).

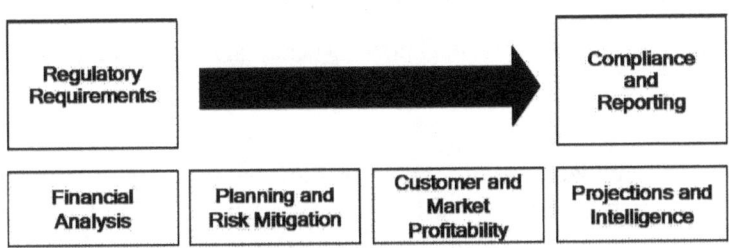

Figure 3.2—Financial Acumen for Realignment

Financial acumen for innovative relevance requires a complex review of interrelated practices, projections, and proposals which not only examines the corporation's health historically, but also examines forward-looking assessments. This could include concentrations, analysis, and comparisons of ROI[xii], net present value, IRR[xiii], top-down budgets, operational risks, credit risks, systemic analysis, and customer partitioned profitability to name, but a few. Gone are the days where vertical segmentation of skills allowed a leader to rise up and run a corporation after starting in the mailroom. Within the global markets, an integration of skills must be melded together to form a foundation for the application of innovatively-relevant solutions.

Foundational items which must be addressed in this area of realignment scrutiny begin with (see Appendices for in-depth financial baselining):

- Is the financial planning process carried out in a meaningful timeframe?

- Is the financial planning process integrated into the business planning process? Are these processes fully documented?

- What is the direct and indirect costs of the process and associated sub-processes?

- Are process owners clearly identified?

- Are there procedures for the incorporation of feedback built into the processes for corrections and adjustments?

- Is the financial planning process actively communicated to the appropriate personnel?

- Are personnel trained and educated on the use of and need for proper financial planning? Use of corporate financial processes? Adherence to stated financial procedures and controls?

- Can the accuracy of the data be statistically measured and enhanced?

Without a formalized and adequate framework of financial measures and processes by which to establish a baseline (see Chapter 5), identify problem areas (see Chapter 6), and evaluate progress (see Chapter 7), the financial rationale and implications of your investment and its value to your business, will more likely reflect your wishful thinking than actual reality. We're not talking about a budget or a financial statement, but a foundational investment and operational analysis needed to determine key opportunities and efforts that will be part of the innovative relevance realignment process.

Cross-domain

To achieve a suitable perspective on the efforts needed to diagnose and transform the organization, an individual with cross-domain team expertise should be sought after and secured. This requirement is due to the portability and cross-fertilization of ideas from various industry segments which can benefit your organization. Many times, teams or leaders who are inexperienced with industries outside of their historical disciplines (*e.g.*, investment banking), fail to leverage the practices, results, and lessons learned from others. Typically, this is referred to as the "not-invented-here" syndrome. Without the employment of cross-domain experience, results tend to be vertically based and similar to those undertaken by competitors.

Nevertheless, by applying cross-domain experiential data and lessons, your organization will quickly benefit not only by learning from others mistakes, but by jump-starting the efforts needed to secure the realignment profits. This provides an open-knowledge format that can greatly assist with the determination of accurate financial metrics, technologies, processes, and skill sets required for successful program completions. Moreover, it creates a foundation for the innovative relevance leaders to promote their cohesive realignment agendas with less rework and adjustments.

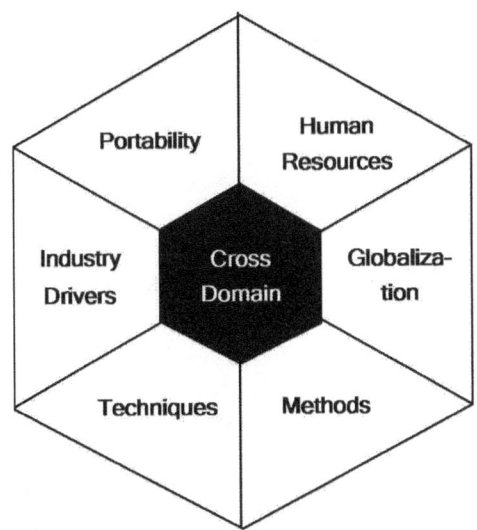

Figure 3.3—Leveraging Cross-Domain Lessons Learned

Three areas of particular value to today's realignment teams are globalization, methods, and techniques (see *Figure 3.3*).

Globalization: Critical to a proper balance of workforce applicability, costs, skills, and delivery schedules. Over 20 years of models and disciplined cross-training processes and procedures exists. See Chapter 9 for a comprehensive discussion of the options available to the program teams.

Methods: These "self-contained" processes continue to be refined within vertical disciplines of telecommunications, healthcare, financial services, information technology, and manufacturing, to name a few. These methods (e.g., Six Sigma, lean manufacturing, capability maturity model, ISO 9000) all have profound significance for the realignment efforts, as they each have unique implications when applied to vertical industry segments. Proceed with care by adopting just the most beneficial methods, rather than using them as a "cookbook" to be applied to all circumstances.

Techniques: Techniques are traditionally portable regardless of the industry with minor modifications. These would include multivariate statistical analysis, regression algorithms, arrival rates, queuing theory, market segmentation, branding, sales analysis, IT delivery processes, and many others.

Operational leadership

Innovative relevance is sustained with results. Results that must be accepted by customers, alliance members, personnel, and trading partners. Bottom-line effects are achieved with the acceptance of realignment initiatives. Operational leadership can make or break your organizational realignment. It can sustain a current enterprise initiative, it can open new global markets, and it can enhance the customer experience which promotes repeat business.

Operational leaders ask the questions that are seldom answered by the multitude of consultants, vendors, and executives. How are we going to solve the value equations with the programs being proposed? Can the initiatives, driven by a strong set of principles and objectives, be sustained if setbacks occur? Who is going to manage the interdependencies and resource competition inherent within the organizational culture? Where will we be 3-, 6-, and 12- months from now, if we utilize the various contingency scenarios that exist? Moreover, what are we precisely going to deliver and when? Will the realignment live up to the expectations of the corporation, the people (we always forget about the people), the customers, the directors, and the shareholders?

Operational leadership starts with the determination and articulation of key processes and associated characteristics:

- Are important operational functions recognized and organized?

- Are relations and communications good among the various operating departments?

- Are the functions logically grouped and aligned to successfully and efficiently control operations?

- Are the functions properly placed so that they can perform without conflict and without crossing organizational boundaries?

- Are the principal functions distributed so that no one operation can dominate without suitable checks and balances?

- Do departments and divisions receive required support from senior management necessary to achieve the assigned objectives?

- Does the organizational chart provide an accurate representation of assigned responsibilities and lines of authority?

- Does the current degree of organizational functional distribution (*i.e.*, centralized, decentralized, distributive) appear suitable?

- Have the roles and responsibilities of assigned staff been clearly stated and incorporated into their performance evaluations?

- Is the organization structured to further the objectives of the company?

- Does the organizational structure provide for sustainability and consistency of operations?

- Is the organization exhibiting signs of dysfunctionality in key product lines? Processes? Customer relations?

- Are there formal procedures for written communications within the company? For verbal communications? For electronic distributions?

Once attributed, as detailed in the supporting appendices, these items establish the foundation for experienced projections, programs, and IT initiatives.

IT knowledge

A critical element of accepting and utilizing the rationale and implications of innovative relevance programs is a solid technological foundation. Very few corporations have a clear focus of the impact technology decisions produce on the bottom line, or the effect alterations will have on the methods of conducting business. Too often, IT alternatives are presented with brief background materials on the IRR, NPV[xiv], cost savings and avoidance for a multi-million dollar investment that provides "competitive advantage." In fact, a lack of comprehension has significantly contributed to "rubber stamp" approvals for numerous ill-conceived decisions, which have never produced any advantage (see *Figure 3.4*—experiential data confirms that between 60% and 80% of IT efforts fail to deliver projected returns or meet stated timeframes).

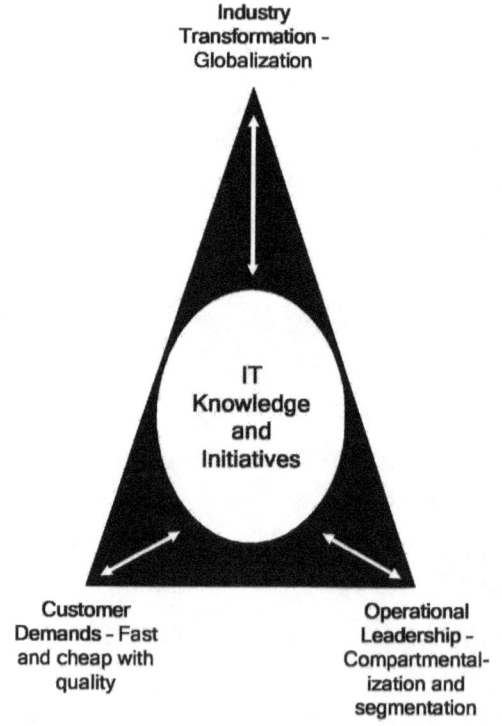

Figure 3.4—Triple Pressures Changing IT Knowledge

Securing the broad-based experience in this segment is sometimes very confusing and filled with trial and error. Due to the specialized nature and certification programs[xv] sponsored by competing and sometimes contentious industry groups, personnel skills are usually very limited and not broad based for realignment initiatives. Furthermore, with the globalization and disenfranchisement of IT workers, the depth and commitment of domestic experience has been severely limited.

- Are objectives established for each of the IT disciplines?

- Are processes developed and implemented to optimize objectives while improving the usage of information?

- Are there measurements in place to quantify the value of customer and web delivery systems?

- Are there policies in place which support organizational principles and technology selections?

- Do policies address security and business continuance for critical delivery systems?

- Do the policies address customer access to informational data stores? Their dissemination? Privacy?

- Are explanations of variances in plan-to-actual status included in the reports?

- Are external resources utilized for technology research, intellectual capital, and program delivery?

- Are funding sources identified whenever they are outside the normal budgeting process or specifically tied to a project?

- Are cost and profit estimates compared with actual results after products are delivered?

- Are periodic evaluations made of existing product lines with regard to marketshare and volumes?

- Is there a systematic analysis and evaluation of customer preferences for products, services, and technologies?

Striving for the appropriate usage of technology (*i.e.*, hardware, software, services, and process) is a key enabler to corporate success—your success. Therefore, we will comprehensively examine the IT function in subsequent chapters, while Appendices C and D provide detailed review criteria that can assist the realignment leader with relevance determinations needed for correct investment decisions.

Corporations constantly employ new methods to streamline operations and improve productivity. We know these disciplines in many forms, including: Six Sigma, BPR, strategic sourcing, CMM[xvi], Balanced Scorecard, and many others. Yet it is exceedingly uncommon for an executive committee to review the implications of these items from a holistic viewpoint. To be more precise, most improvements brought to senior management are classically examined in their vertical, compartmentalized silos. Without a comprehensive consideration of the technology and its architectonic effect on the institution, how can the corporation ensure that the investment and changes being approved are actually what benefits the shareholders? When the post-mortems of the recent corporate alignment processes are examined, what lessons learned will have significantly contributed to their failures at an early stage?

Program management with process integration

Experienced project management personnel are probably the most readily available of the innovative relevance skills to acquire. However, these skills by themselves are of little value to the realignment leader. These must be combined with the other critical skill and experiential areas to create the proper disposition and maturity required to successfully execute a corporate realignment.

It should also be noted that an individual with project management skills or certifications is not a program manager. Certifications are valuable to enable an employer to find qualified individuals who are trained or experienced in techniques or methods. Program managers are typically those individuals who are responsible for efforts in excess of $15 million USD and project teams exceeding 150 concurrent personnel. Program experience is about the simultaneous management of many projects all integrated into a cohesive whole to produce an end-result (see *Figure 3.5*).

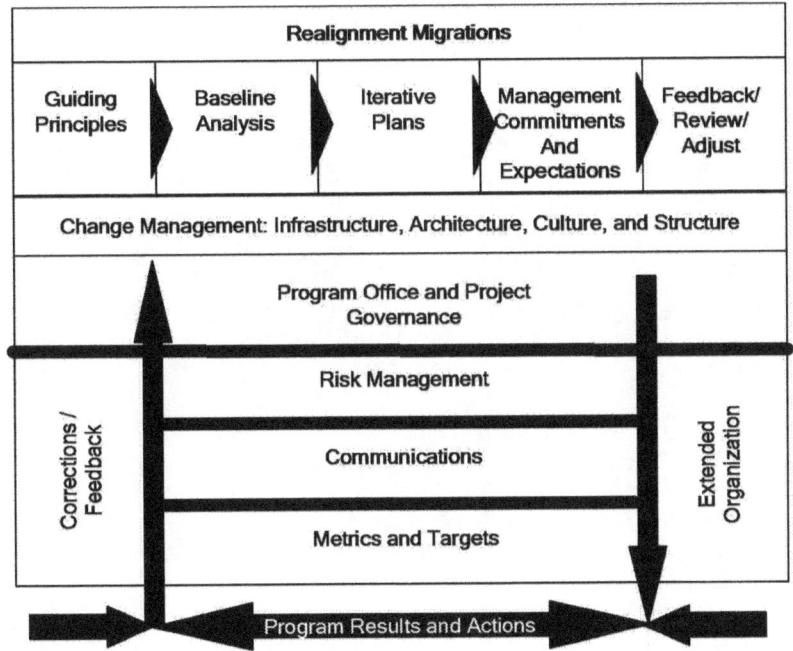

Figure 3.5—Program Management Overview

Program managers are familiar with business process management, process mapping and can assess the value of inputs, outputs, and information exchange between organizational entities to quickly determine their value both quantitatively and qualitatively. Program managers typically analyze results and problems using three-dimensional models for scope, quality, and costs. These multi-dimensional models are linked to other "cubes" to analytically determine the best course of action under the current circumstances. Experience makes a program manager—not certifications. Multidisciplinary models, methods, and techniques are what they provide your organization. They usually represent less than 1%[xvii] of advertised "program managers" within the United States and a much lower percentage internationally.

The use of tools in this area of specialization includes robust program office software, business intelligence cubes, process redesign and mapping, resource reporting, and project management methods. On the other hand, before money is allocated for tracking and management, a few initial questions need to be asked:

- Will formalized realignment program processes be utilized for the innovative relevance initiatives?

- Are adjustments to the formal realignment program processes routinely communicated to the required stakeholder groups?

- Are there unmistakable owners of the process and sub-processes?

- Are the formal realignment program processes applied consistently within the stakeholder groups?

- Is there a formal process which routinely reviews management principles, models, and standards?

- Do methods and techniques exist to incorporate statistical feedback into the review process for reassessment?

- Do regular reviews of processes exist which evaluate the relevance of the realignment programs, and the accuracy of the information sourced or generated?

- Are the processes which routinely track and communicate program measurements, generally accessible to the stakeholders and supporting teams?

Program management is essential for all successful innovative relevance implementations. A critical success factor is to find personnel that possess cross-domain experience who can mitigate the risks and uncertainty introduced by the realignment's programs.

Lessons learned

A leader or team that lacks experience with realignments can cost the organization profits and program results. Innovative relevance initiatives demand program, not project, level techniques and methods. Cross-domain industry knowledge will be critical to provide the "out-of-box" thinking needed for fast-paced and demanding realignments.

- Leaders must be skilled in globalization. There is no substitute for this critical skill set as it will impact alternative decisions during program startup and on-going operational management.

- Financial acumen demands complex and sometimes loose associations with non-financial primitive metrics (*i.e.*, financial results may be the "effect" being measured, but are these being "caused" by non-financial events or actions?)

- Regulatory and compliance needs will be critical to accepting the operational risks and for the accurate tracking and reporting of realignment program efforts.

- IT knowledge must be broad based and not concentrated on a single vertical discipline or application.

- Operational leadership and experience dealing with alliances, partners and joint ventures will be needed to provide the integration touchpoints for extended organizational acceptance of program goals.

- Experienced program personnel needed for realignment efforts represent a very unique skill set, but their capabilities significantly reduce operational and systemic risks.

- Personalities and styles will have a great deal to do with experienced personnel success in realignment efforts. Due diligence to ensure acceptability for the "future model" (discussed at length in Chapter 6) must be performed. Selecting program managers to meet the current state models (see Chapter 5) will result in experienced personnel who can be limiting factors for innovative realignment efforts.

Chapter 4

Engage the Extended Organization
Sustaining the Innovative Relevance team environment

Organizational Commitment. Sounds simple enough? Yet, this key cornerstone for realignment efforts is many times left to chance during the iterative migration steps necessary for sustained transformation (see Chapter 7). A great deal of time and procedural effort is spent on securing the initial funding, fervor of intent, and marketing the potential outcomes to executive management and their staffs. However, when we examine the results of a comprehensive realignment effort, we can consistently recognize the failure of the teams and organizations to understand the variability and criticality of sustainable commitment. Sustainability of multifaceted realignments demands identification and perseverance in five essential areas.

Understand your culture

Every organization has an established culture. A defacto culture exists whether we have an unambiguous comprehension of it or not. Organizational cultures exist from the smallest mom-and-pop store to the largest multinational conglomeration employing thousands. It can be described as conservative, risk taking, stodgy, inept, stellar, innovative, objective driven, unfocused, profitable, collaborative, diverse, methodical, chaotic, or customer-driven. Yet, it is the combination of these classifications that create opportunity and turmoil for realignment initiatives.

Organizational culture is what guides the aggressiveness of migration strategies, projects, and programs. This culture can work to the benefit of the initiatives or act like a hurricane for horticulturists growing cactuses in the desert. The evolution of culture is not an overnight event. It can take many months and will likely be as a result of significant management adjustments and/or personnel reassignments. Cultural characteristics contribute explicitly and implicitly to the implementation risks found within many innovative relevance programs. Let's examine a very simplified example to highlight the thought processes necessary, for ensuring an accurate fit of realignment initiatives when mapping these against an existing or projected organizational culture.

Sonya was a senior vice president. At 38 years old, she had risen rapidly into prominence within a financial services organization. She was known for her effective usage of customer facing business and marketing methods to reach out and improve cross-selling to the existing customer base. She was technically proficient and a strategic thinker.

As part of a recent reorganization, her operational team went from a handful to over 120. The personnel she inherited averaged 18 years of tenure, had survived four mergers, and were known for their lack of cooperation. These employees represented the traditional organizational culture of the enterprise. Nevertheless, she immediately saw the potential opportunities for the organization, and undertook realignment initiatives to improve operational efficiencies, while expanding market share with new products and promotions.

Sonya secured executive commitment for her initiatives and started out with unmistakable fervor on the tasks, which were scheduled to conclude over an 11-month period. As they approached the fourth month of the realignment, it became clear something had gone wrong. The initiatives were "locked-up" in meetings, passive-aggressive hostility was being experienced, and the costs were exceeding the targets.

Upon closer inspection of the results and dysfunctionality, it was concluded that the realignment initiatives were far too progressive for the organizational culture. The changes being demanded coupled with the modifications needed in behavior and attitude could not be obtained within the current organizational climate. Alterations in rewards, reporting, communication, collaboration, roles and responsibilities all had to be made before the programs could be successful. The programs were correct, but the organizational environment and undocumented processes were pushing the efforts further into the "As-Is" bureaucratic culture.

As a result, Sonya made several critical adjustments including more time for education and training, key personnel changes, and use of iterative programs so that the realignment could take place in more organizationally "acceptable transition bites." This situation added three months to her timeline given her need to "stop-start." Had she recognized this earlier, the timeframes and goals would have been met using the original schedule.

Organizational culture must not be underestimated. The ability of a realignment effort to meet its stated objectives will be contingent upon the organization's ability to accept and execute the modifications. A stellar plan and comprehensive approach means little if the organization lacks the ability to act upon it. Risk mitigation strategies can improve the probabilities of success, but they cannot eliminate the potential negative consequences for an organization that doesn't want to be realigned.

Engage "touchpoints"

"Touchpoints" is a common term and model used within the IT application world. This concept has relevance with our ability to prepare innovative realignment strategies and initiatives. A touchpoint should be thought of as any interaction, interdependency, or informational need that spans departments, divisions, or organizations (in the case of alliances or partners). Realignment efforts that cross boundaries will require the support of these entities and the people contained within them.

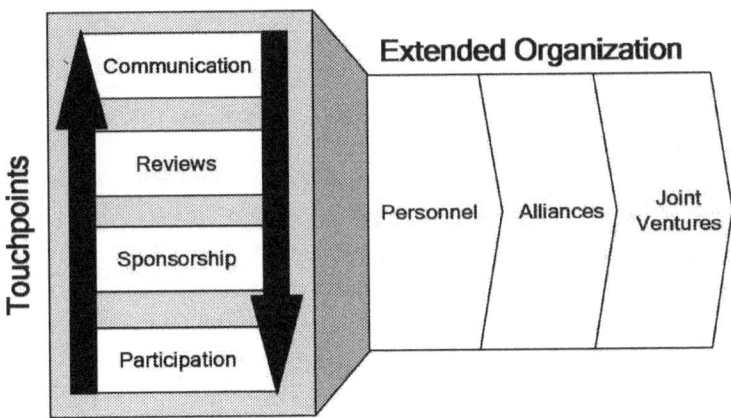

Figure 4.1—Realignment Collaboration

The global business climate has necessitated the utilization of collaborative arrangements that span time zones, cultures, and localized processes. These linkages create risks for failure, yet can improve the timelines for success. The "reaching out" to the extended organization can include (see *Figure 4.1*):

Communications: Most groups that are affected will require some involvement or participation in the realignment efforts to protect their interests. Their lack of participation and appreciation can create missed timeframes, ill-will, and lost profits.

Reviews: Conduct assessment reviews with stakeholder parties to capture their input, solicit assistance, and make them part of the solutions. If used properly, their reviews can reduce risks, errors, and speed the time to delivery.

Sponsorships: Depending upon the projected results of the realignment, you may want to solicit senior touchpoint personnel as "niche-based" sponsors. Their leadership in compartmentalized initiatives can provide the much needed visibility, support, and cross-domain expertise required to guarantee realignment sustainability and delivery quality.

Participation: It is improbable that realignment programs will be solely contained within a discrete area or division. As a result, you will find the need to engage "extended" resources who will be required to actively participate in the innovative relevance initiatives.

The inclusion of touchpoint organizations can strongly promote realignment efforts. Incorporation of their organizations should be viewed positively, as experienced realignment practitioners realize the value promoted by multiple stakeholders. On the other hand, there may be circumstances when these touchpoint relationships can be liabilities.

Touchpoint liabilities occur when organizations and/or personnel refuse to accept the need for transformation and realignment. In these cases, early efforts must concentrate on their identification, and suitable mitigation strategies must be developed and approved by executive management. Touchpoints also need to address unique participants that include alliances and joint ventures.

Alliances and joint ventures

As part of the extended organizational family, alliances and partnerships present some unique challenges and opportunities. The opportunities present themselves in the form of additional resources, cost deferments, risk mitigations (operational, credit, systemic), customer facing, and speed to market. The challenges arise with profit sharing (if they are deferring costs, expect a desire to share in the gains), complexity, political maneuvering, cultural clashes, and longer lead and delivery timeframes.

Regardless of the contractual legal requirements and personal feelings about how each relationship affects your overall timeframes and goal obtainment, your most productive route is to anticipate their needs in advance. These may include:

Approvals: Depending upon the profit potentials and legal liabilities, they may demand to be part of the decision process.

Requirements Inclusion: Contingent upon the relationships, it will be necessary to integrate the realignment programs with the processes and procedures which support customer delivery, product support, manufacturing, and distribution, to name but a few.

Regulatory Validation: If the realignment has a potential to influence the numerous organizational regulations that are due to industry or government requirements, there will be a demand to obtain validation before any approvals are granted. They may require third-party confirmation for any actions which would affect the relationship.

Compliance: With regulatory requirements, compliance processes, procedures, and standards, must be adhered to and maintained. Record retention and/or information capture could be critical to the partner and joint venture relationship.

Financial Impact: When profits are on the line, participating organizations usually require an audit or management consulting opinion on the realignment's costs/benefit analysis. This will be used as a "safety valve" in the event reality does not meet expectations (see Chapter 12). Periodic validations may also be required, depending upon the total duration and risks of the realignment.

> **Board Delivery**: Based upon the complexity, impact, and liability potentials, you may be expected to interact directly with the partner's or joint venture's board. Highly visible efforts have been known to submit changes to audit or technology review committees monthly or quarterly. Due to ever increasing personal and professional liabilities combined with shareholder suits, this practice is becoming widely accepted to understand the total risks being assumed by the partner or joint venture relationship.

While most realignment efforts will have limited involvement from a partner or joint venture (there could be multiple), proper planning and investigation is required to reduce risks of failures or re-launches.

Continuous visibility

To protect and provide continuous support for innovative realignment efforts, there must be continual communication regarding the progress (positive and negative) of the efforts. Historically, migration initiatives would begin with great fanfare, extensive visibility, and moving speeches. As time progresses, the "newness" or commonality of the events moves the criticality of efforts away from the forefront of organizational communications and reporting. The programs become buried within the monthly and quarterly events, lost to obscurity and importance.

Visibility requires several components:

> **Disciplined Processes**: To achieve consistent and regular information to track and report progress, a series of integrated processes must be established before realignment efforts are inaugurated. This will minimally include tracking "saves," financial benefits, resources, time reporting, status reports, RYG (red, yellow, green) analysis, exceptions, task completion, change and issue management.
>
> **Training**: While the establishment of processes are step one, training on their usage becomes the next critical component. Personnel must understand acceptable levels of completion, data types, information availability, privacy, security, escalations, and where to go for help.

Dashboards and Scorecards: To ensure that meaningful information needed for timely decision making is compiled, pre-established reports and data relationships must be modeled and approved before their usage is required. These reports will not only utilize the data, but establish control limits for deviation, cause-to-effect, and anomalies that meet no known criteria. Critical to the predetermination of these scorecards are success criteria—how do we know we've met the requirements, objectives, and goals set forth in Chapter 1? These scorecards and dashboards are representations of the migration or end-states. Multivariate analysis, statistical testing, and linear regression techniques may also be employed as warranted for program examination.

Information Availability: Reporting, dashboards, and meetings, must be made available to those who have a vested interest in the outcome of the realignment. While this can be the largest and most ambiguous decision for key sponsors, it cannot be taken lightly. Distrust, passive-aggressiveness, and wasted cycle-time can be avoided with accurate information flows supported by materially significant data sources. The failure to provide information needed to promote visibility can contribute substantial risks to the programs, while increasing costs and diminishing desired benefits (*i.e.*, time, quality, and costs).

The job of ensuring continuous visibility should be entrusted starting in month one to a dedicated person or team (depending upon the size), whose sole responsibilities are to gather, compile, and communicate required information. Methods of delivery could be hardcopy, e-mail, or web sites. These can be supported by a host of off-the-shelf software and organizations who can quickly import standardized processes to reduce startup time and costs. Ongoing maintenance should also be a factor in any decisions due to the costs of making changes, portability and, of course, personnel retraining (you will have initiative members make departures or additions).

Organizational dysfunctionality

While this is a topic we will cover in depth in Chapter 15, most impediments originate from a lack of organizational commitment. This dysfunctionality manifests itself in chaotic forms of business disillusionment, personnel dissatisfaction, and organizational rejection of the realignment programs and results. At various stages of the realignment's lifecycle, different personnel and groups will become dysfunctional and hinder the progress and pace of transformation. These challenging actions are normal. Experience requires that you do not overreact to the opposition placed in front of the programs too negatively, or you may risk losing commitment and assistance needed for subsequent tasks.

Organizations are fundamentally comprised of people and processes. The uncertainty created by applying innovative relevance to realignment initiatives generates ill-will, apprehension, aggressiveness, hostility, rejection, empowerment, apathy, resignation, loathing, and joy to name a few. Every person and the processes which make their job functions meaningful are affected in unique and sometimes material ways. Therefore, to assist with the identification and management of this certainty, realignment leaders must promote and embrace training and education, in addition to the possibility of personnel reassignments and separations (see Chapter 8). In most circumstances, the latter actions should be used sparingly. Nevertheless, there is always some attrition and separations that are required to promote the on-going health of the realignment migrations.

Lessons learned

To effectively obtain the required support needed from suppliers, alliance members, and joint ventures to sustain the innovative relevance programs, you must actively integrate these extended stakeholders into the realignment processes. The techniques and methods chosen for collaboration will depend upon your own organizational culture and risk tolerances.

- Continual communication will be critical to promoting trust, understanding, and involvement.

- Participation from extended organizations can be very valuable when assigned to definitive program actions and reviews.

- Involvement from extended participants must be approved by the realignment sponsors before they are engaged. Their subsequent involvement will require the team to assign them definitive roles and responsibilities.

- Regulatory validation and approval may be required. Solicit responses from industry groups or self-regulating organizations to determine required approval processes and lead times.

- With organizations adopting greater board level independence, it is recommended that the program teams engage the corporate board as a means to reduce the potential of litigation, organizational resistance, and failure. Boards can be useful for checkpoint reviews, confirmations, and strategic directions needed to guide and sustain the realignment programs.

- Information reporting and collection cannot be underestimated. The establishment of dashboards and scorecards will provide a consistent and continuous portal into the performance of the realignment programs.

SECTION 2

IDENTIFY THE NEED— CREATE THE PLANS

"If you wish to understand a philosopher, do not ask what he says, but find out what he wants."

—Nietzsche

Nietzsche addresses a fatal flaw within numerous realignment initiatives. Too often practitioners fail to define the fundamental needs that drive the efforts relegating their activities to a series of short-term gains with long-term declines. The chapters within this segment form the blueprint for the creation of self-sustaining programs that are driven by definitive business requests.

| Baseline and Confirm | Go? | Assess and Project | Go? | Iterative Migration |

Innovative Relevance Process Essentials

Within this section, we'll establish the requirements and frameworks for assessment necessary to conduct the realignment, while promoting accurate innovative relevance decision making. This section is further supported by detailed appendices, providing the "how-to" and mechanics of conducting the innovative relevance realignment.

Chapter 5: Baseline and Confirm

Chapter 6: Assess and Project

Chapter 7: Iterative Migration

Chapter 5

Baseline and Confirm
Without a roadmap, any path will suffice

Every journey has a beginning. For innovative relevance, its itinerary starts with a concrete awareness of the current situation or "As-Is" model. This requirement is founded in the simple tenet of "leverage"—current processes, personnel, customers, technologies, findings, observations, reports, regulations, information, facilities, or investments.

Corporations constantly employ new methods to streamline operations and improve productivity. We know these disciplines in many forms including, Six Sigma, BPR, strategic sourcing, CMM, Balanced Scorecard, and many others. Yet, it is exceedingly uncommon for an organization to review the implications of these items from an innovative relevance standpoint. To be more precise, most improvements brought to the organization are classically examined within their vertical, compartmentalized benefits. Without an unambiguous consideration of the technology and its architectonic effect on the institution, how can the executives ensure that the investment and changes being approved are actually what benefits the shareholders, personnel, and profit potentials? When the post-mortems of the recent corporate failures are examined, what misunderstood relevant processes will have significantly contributed to their failures at an initial phase?

To effectively realign the organization, you must know where to begin. A "snapshot" of the strengths and weaknesses must be completed objectively and expediently. This baseline must be performed to determine the current problems, symptoms, and causes of the organizational chaos, so that the correct resources and priorities can be given to the innovative relevance programs. Without this baseline, an appropriate migration approach cannot be created to meet the needs of the organization, customers, alliances, and employees (see *Figure 5.1*).

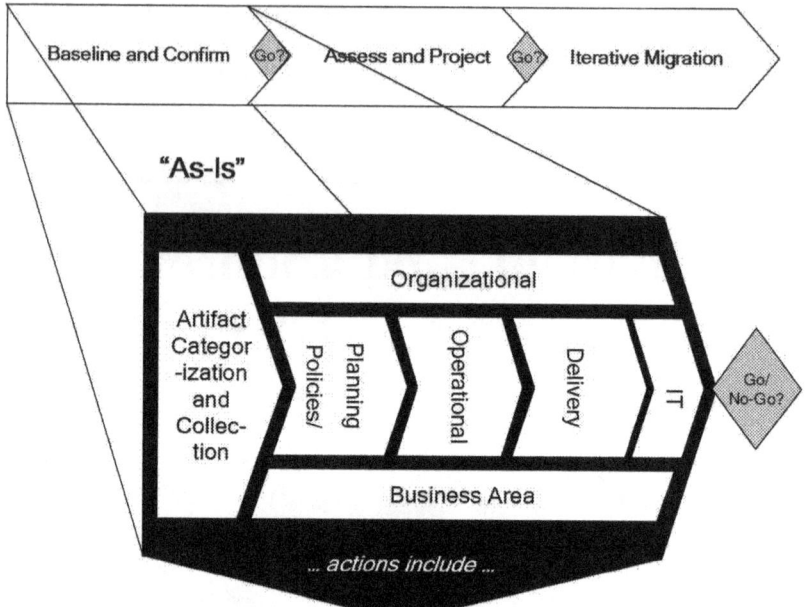

Figure 5.1—The Baseline Model

The baseline process is characterized as the industry, business, organizational, and technology drivers that are presently acting upon the organization. These drivers influence decision making, purchases, vendor alliances, markets, product introductions, measurements, economic, and government regulations. The baseline needs to be scrutinized (see Chapter 6) and projected to ensure that reality meets the perception of the organization and the executive management team. Without a consistent appreciation of the industry, business, organizational, and technology drivers (*i.e.,* your baseline), the realignment effort will conclude with disappointing program results and career aspirations.

Artifact collection and categorization

In simple terms, artifact analysis involves:

> The meticulous collection and integration of organizational, industry, business, and technology drivers, documents, reviews, audits, and results to support the assessment and projection of realignment programs (see *Figure 5.2*).

The usage of existing information that contributes to the baseline is often overlooked and many times ignored.

A wealth of top-quality work exists within any organization. While I agree that every item initially collected must be looked at skeptically, its value can be easily confirmed. This confirmation process represents a fraction of the effort needed to acquire new information from scratch. Furthermore, don't discount external reports or informational sources when compiling the artifacts. These sources may provide glimpses of the root causes of prior failures and lost opportunities. If your organization is part of a self-regulating industry or has stringent government regulatory needs, many times this information is critical in assembling the foundation for a comprehensive baseline. If properly catalogued and synthesized, the collection of multiple artifacts can confirm or discount their usefulness.

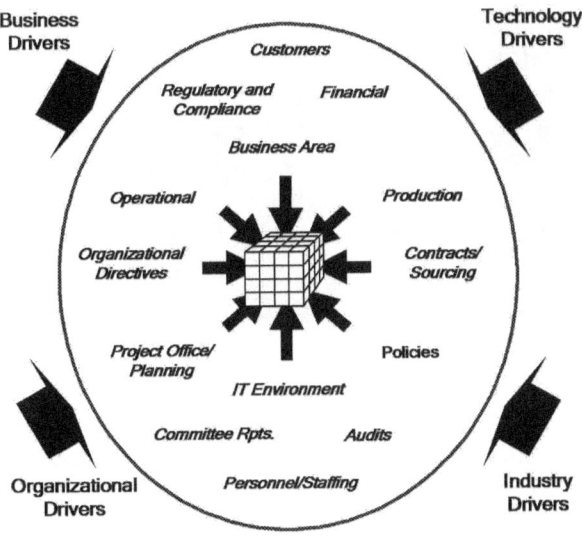

Figure 5.2—Artifact Sourcing

Listed below are some standard examples of informational sources for baseline collection and categorization:

Industry Sources: Government regulations, technological drivers, traditional competition, non-traditional competition, community involvement, environmental constraints, demographics, shareholder suits, compliance trends, pending litigation, lobbying, political special interests, global economic conditions, lending programs, and changing methods and processes.

Business Drivers: Personnel, skill sets, organizational culture, traditional and non-traditional markets, core competencies, plans and investment strategies, mergers and acquisitions, financial targets, market strategies, customer segmentations, board-level committees, program management offices, production schedules, capital investments, operating costs, workforce globalization, and profitability measurements.

Information Technology: Key sources of information include operational schedules, personnel, applications, data sources and uses, methods and techniques (e.g., CMM, Rational), ERP, CRM, call/contact centers, dashboards, help desks, audit reports (internal and external), compliance systems, business intelligence, data warehouses, web services, web sites, customer accesses, and training/mentoring programs.

Organizational: Reporting relationships, segment profitability, outsourcing, critical programs, planning methods, budgeting processes, functional divisions, contingency planning, disaster preparedness, policies, principles, procedures, standards, disclosures, communication methods, marketing programs, investor relations, analysts disclosures, positions, human resources, mergers, acquisitions, joint ventures, alliances, product cycles, customer cycles, seasonality, internal controls, and research and development.

The compilation of this information, once logged, can then be broken down into their distinct data components to assist with the measurement of organization sophistication and maturity (see appendices for measurement and quantification criteria).

As mentioned earlier, this effort is all about creating a "snapshot" of the "As-Is" environment—you're not writing War and Peace. The creation of the baseline requires a laser focus to understand and provide the foundation for realignment launch initiatives. "As-Is" events should be undertaken using a "time boxed" program management approach. This baselining stage should only continue for a set duration (*e.g.*, 30-, 60-, or 90-days). What you and your innovative relevance teams are doing is managing the triple constraints that face any organization—time, quality, scope. When using a fixed duration, we are telling everyone involved, "time is urgent and we are going to include as much as we can within this time framework." Since quality cannot be compromised, the only variable factor is scope. "Time boxing" creates a sense of urgency and criticality for the entire organization, including trading partners and alliance members.

The last item to be addressed in this subsection is the use of interviews, focusing sessions, and group facilitation seminars. While each of these data gathering approaches has more applicability in some circumstances than others, they can be overused in the early stages of realignment. Some teams and leaders believe that these are the "best practices" when it comes to conducting baseline sourcing. These techniques are highly applicable in the second half of the time box effort. While you will be required to interact with others to gather the sourcing documents, engaging in dialogues to collect or confirm facts when you do not have a basis for comparison (for your preliminary data gathering activities) can be fraught with danger. These "ungrounded" discussions can unduly influence data collection methods, usage, and personal perceptions. They should be minimized during the first half of the artifact collection and categorization stage.

Organizational (see detailed criteria in Appendix A)[xviii]

An organizational baseline is the most familiar and straightforward. To ascertain the robustness of processes, procedures, and policies, artifacts from the representative functional areas need to be collected. Example enterprise artifacts (shown in Figure 5.3) can be utilized for derivation of organizational maturity, interrelationships, duplication of efforts, and overall operational, credit, and systemic risks.

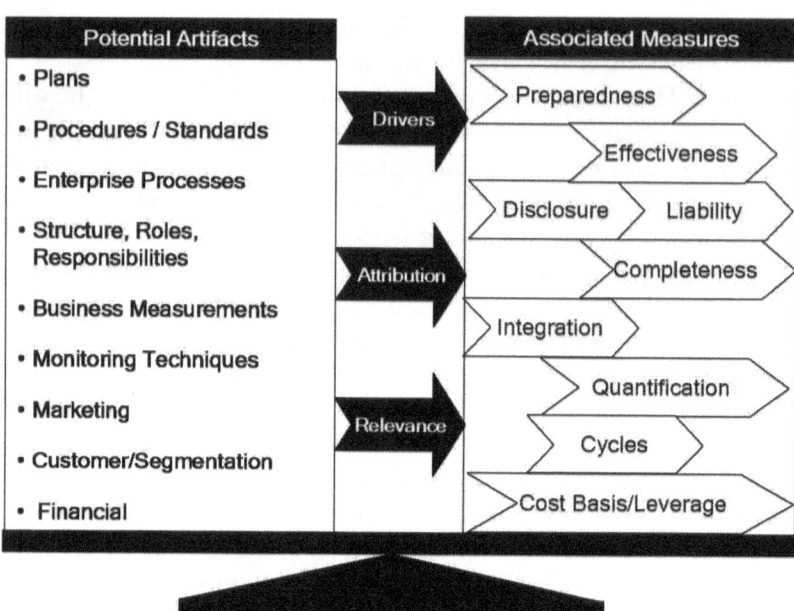

Figure 5.3—Organizational Criteria

Planning: Baselining in this area examines operational, tactical, and strategic planning, financial measures, statements, and profitability, goals, objectives, and strategies by line of business, organizational reporting, measures, and formalized relationships.

Policies and Structure: Functional articulation and active management, issue and conflict resolution, HR, integration with corporate goals and profit objectives, dissemination and assimilation, compliance and regulatory retention, conflicts of interest, and all phases within line and staff business functions.

Alliances and Joint Ventures: Identification of processes, owners, and measurements. Additionally, how are alliances and joint ventures reviewed for continuous relevance, innovative adoption, and retirement? What statistical or numerical measures are applied to investments, profits, and margins to determine their fully-burdened benefit?

Business area (see detailed criteria in Appendix B)

Concentration now focuses on the individual segments within the organization. These could be self-contained departments or divisions that have significant operating costs, profit generation, or that act as a self-contained business unit (*e.g.,* SBU or line of business). It represents a decomposition of the enterprise so that we understand any anomalies or fragmentation which occurs when we move up and down the organizational entity. Realignment relevance needs to comprehend the interrelationships between the larger entity and those units that have autonomy or dependence to derive profits and results from investments, processes, or product lines.

Artifacts being sought after will include:

- divisional plans,
- operating results,
- capital investments,
- resource loading,
- disciplined analysis and techniques, (*e.g.,* ISO, Six Sigma, lean manufacturing),
- customer feedback and surveys,
- impact analysis on key initiatives,
- conflict resolution,
- staffing,
- prioritizations,
- needs identification and analysis, and
- market opportunities.

These artifacts and their confirmation using multiple sources, allows the team to assemble a thorough blueprint of existing operational practices, while pointing to early findings and observations that can be useful for short-term improvement efforts. Short-term efforts, when used in conjunction with the other areas of analysis, can assist the realignment leaders with the realization of benefits sooner. These activities can be started in parallel, with the remaining phases of realignment, as they will be self-contained, have high payback, and represent a low risk for the organization and team.

Information Technology—IT (see detailed criteria in Appendices C, D, and E)

Information technology has been clouded in mystique since its inception. In the 1960's and 1970's, IT was run by a group of scientists who communicated with machines in odd and cryptic dialects (they called them programming languages). In the 1980's, we witnessed a quantum shift in strategy, with the creation of the Apple Computer Corporation and an idea borrowed from consumer electronics where, like the radio, everyone should have their own "personal computer." As the 1980's progressed and the 1990's appeared, computer numerical controlled (CNC) machinery became common place in production lines and on shop floors. We witnessed our farming friend from earlier chapters, being forced to deal with GPS[xix] planting techniques, microprocessor enhanced implements, and a new economic reality of "invest or be left behind." No industry was spared from the mantra of technological revolution.

As we neared the new millennium, we were faced with an apocalyptic scenario of technology—unresponsive financial markets, economic turmoil, military policing actions, and the list went on. We invested unprecedented sums of money in machines, software, personnel, outsourcing relationships, and business continuance services. We now know that while the concern was valid, the effects and hype generated by industry analysts, IT soothsayers, research groups, and our own employees was exaggerated.

It is with this backdrop of technological ebb and flow, which we need to concentrate a significant portion of our baseline, to appreciate the needs and benefits being achieved by our investments. While the mantra of the new millennium is about ERP systems, "know thy customer[xx]," business process management, offshore outsourcing, and declining IT workers, we need to recognize the critical impacts that technology decisions have on our daily operations, production capacity, and profitability. The foundation for realignment transformation is NOT about technology, but technology is an enabler for our marketing strategy, product roll-outs, and globalization initiatives. The relevance of these investments, processes, and their organizational impact, is what we are going to examine in this baselining effort.

Today we are bombarded with rapidly increasing advancements in wireless delivery of information, vendor consolidations, data access, along with the needs for strong security and personal privacy. Combined with a hostile and uncertain future for personal liberties, religious freedoms, and human rights, the importance of clearly positioning and leveraging our investments in technology takes center stage. Our prior decisions, modes of operation, and organizational acceptance of technology changes, will have a quantifiable effect on our innovative relevance (*i.e.,* our profitability by being able to assimilate and sustain transformation).

To properly frame this baseline, we need to examine seven key areas (see *Figure 5.4*). Each of these classifications brings insight into not only current sophistication and process completeness, but also a knowledge of techniques, tools, and procedures, which can be leveraged for iterative migration activities from the shop floor back into the computing or customer solutions centers (even if they are outsourced).

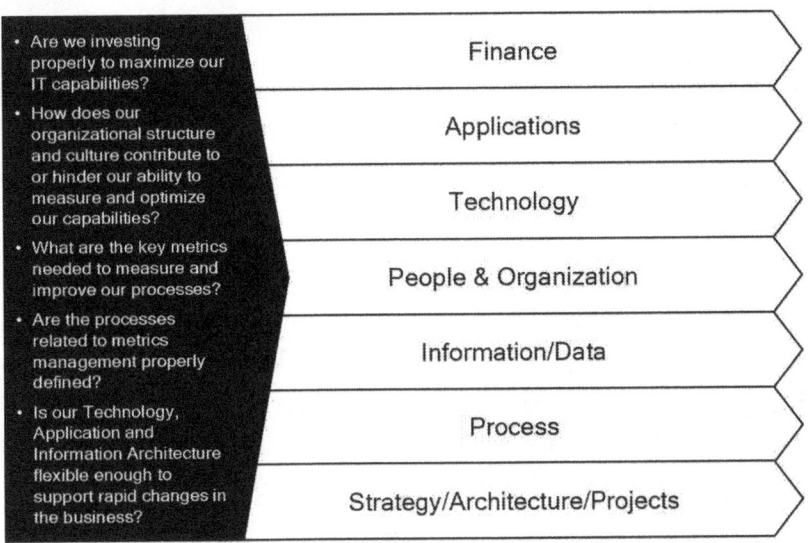

Figure 5.4—Understanding the IT Enablers

Finance: The financial rationale and implications for technology investment continue to be misunderstood. This area will be a critical component to comprehension of the drivers behind investment decisions, outsourcing efforts, education, and retraining.

Applications: The most common and recognizable of all technology baselining efforts. This has been the area of constant investments that have yielded only marginal returns. Applications within a company range from hundreds to tens of thousands and consume an average of over 20% of the annual operating budgets[xxi].

Technology: Technology (*i.e.*, hardware and software) is usually the least stable of the information processing and distribution environment. Efforts in these areas should concentrate on operational impacts, refresh rates, maintenance costs, integration barriers, and error rates.

People & Organization: People and the processes are utilized to manage, communicate, and interact with technology—they are the drivers for profit realization. Therefore, the baseline effort seeks to understand associated planning, procedures, deployment benefits, and consequences.

Information/Data: A critical area for examination. Within highly visible business, customer, and competitive intelligence systems, resides the need for information integrity and sourcing of information. Its origination, manipulation, storage, and disposal are at the center of many prominent litigation efforts, organizational losses, and ruined careers.

Process: Technology efforts support processes that span the corporation. Additionally, technology has created secondary processes that are unique to its management, delivery, and on-going maintenance.

Strategy, Architecture, Projects: Essential to the active management of IT investments, architectural knowledge is a foundation for improvements. Strategies incorporated into this architectonic underpinning provide the much needed and measurable projects that are undertaken to improve productivity, profits, and personnel.

It is imperative that when examining the technology environment, realignment efforts address their holistic usage and deployment. IT should not be viewed as just a department or group when undertaking realignment efforts. Technology has a material effect on all functions within organizations. It starts at the executive offices and continues down to the shop floor. If restricted to only an artificial function or organizational boundary, then the value, and potentially the success, of the innovative relevance activities may result in disappointment.

Operational management (see detailed criteria in Appendices D, E, and F)

Operational management is increasingly based on work flows and processes. From informational flows with value-added activities, we create the measures, metrics, and utilization criteria to assist with efficiency and capacity schedules (see *Figure 5.5*). It's the combination of these components that directly influences the department or divisional profitability.

Furthermore, in this portion of the baseline, we seek to document the resolution activities, contingency measures, and the feedback and adjustment strategies, to determine how the organization corrects for failures and expands for success.

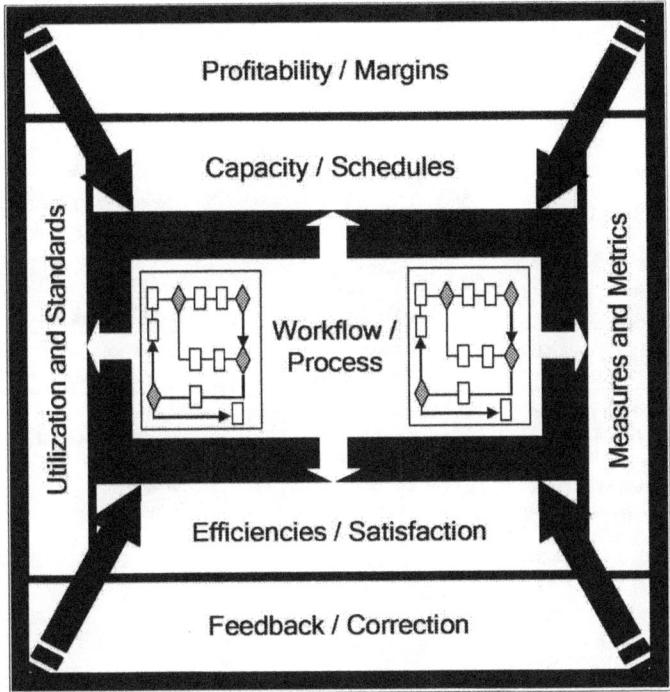

Figure 5.5—Operational Relationships

Depending upon the specific goals and objectives of the realignment programs, this area can be greatly expanded or contracted to meet the schedules and imperatives that face the organization. The appendices cover a great many discrete criteria, so it will be necessary for you to tailor them to meet your requirements.

Delivery review

The final segment for baseline review involves an examination of production delivery, compliance, and organizational sustainability (see *Figure 5.6*). Continuous delivery and quality enhancements are demanded by discerning customers and our need to stay competitive. Expanding and far reaching regulatory requirements coupled with legal mandates are key imperatives, which must be addressed at their provisioning/generating sources. Within the compliance procedures, processes must guarantee security of information, timeliness of access, and conformity to requirements during the production delivery cycles—and not afterwards. Sustainability of delivery and responsibility for problem resolution or operational modifications must be not only defined, but continually reviewed for applicability and conformity to changing business needs.

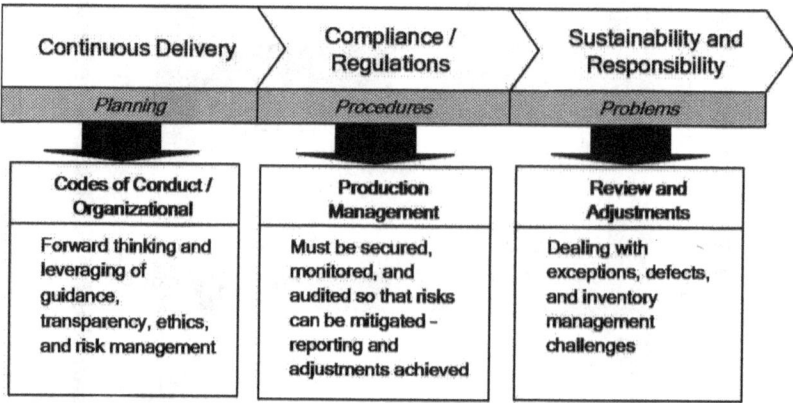

Figure 5.6—Production Distinctiveness

Artifact collection in this stage is typically supported by reports and specialized operational systems that ensure consistency and integration. The absence of automation for these critical areas represents a level of immaturity and manual disciplines that will be hard to sustain, as realignment and growth projections are merged to form the innovative relevance programs. Artifacts in this, or other areas, should be captured in their original electronic form unless you have specific or contrary requirements for discovery, regulatory, or alliance reviews.

Go/No-Go (time for a decision)

Now that we have reached the end of our time box, we've produced our outputs, categorized our work products, and integrated our artifacts. We need to obtain validation of the realignment initiative before any further resources are allocated and spent. This "Go/No-Go" decision point is an opportunity to make mid-course corrections in scope, approaches, principles, or end-states that we identified early on in Chapter 1.

The "As-Is" state confirmation process provides the ideal opportunity for changes in team composition, techniques, and methods as you get ready for the Assess and Project stage (see Chapter 6). These adjustments could be minor or major depending upon the results realized during this fixed duration effort. When placed under pressure and stress, teams and organizations behave differently. It is also a good idea, before you make any adjustments, to utilize the organization's performance review process to objectively evaluate the team member's actions and behaviors. If the organization lacks the processes or disciplines for this type of performance evaluation, there are numerous off-the-shelf employee/team management packages that can be purchased for a nominal amount via the Internet or your local bookstore.

Once you have completed your post review (again, time is of the essence so we are talking about days, not weeks), you are ready to review the results with the sponsors and involved stakeholders. This should be done individually or in small groups before attempting to assemble a larger audience. If there are areas that are sensitive or damaging to a given area or individual, it is important that you have these discussions privately before presenting your findings to the larger audience. You gain very little from a "public flogging" within a corporate arena as these same individuals may become critical to improvement programs in later stages.

When you have obtained the approvals, necessary adjustments, and any additional funding, you are now ready to begin the next phase of the innovative relevance realignment—Assess and Project.

Lessons learned

The basics are in place. You have the experience. You have secured the correct support, and you've aligned your extended organization to match the culture of the enterprise. Coupled with the establishment of the vision and supporting principles, you are ready to begin the journey towards the future profit models.

- Artifact sourcing and collection must be meticulously used within preset "time boxes" to instill a sense of urgency and completeness.

- Sources of artifacts include organizational, business, industry, and technological.

- Sourced artifacts must be integrated and synthesized to form baseline informational cubes (see Chapter 11) that can be analyzed during the fit-gap stage (see Chapter 6).

- Production delivery processes and procedures must be gathered to assist with current and future projections. Additionally, these must also be understood to guarantee day-to-day customer and delivery requirements, while the transformation efforts are underway (see Chapter 14).

- Exceptions, metrics, and measures must be collected during the baselining efforts to assist with environmental complexity, regulatory requirements, and financial controls.

Chapter 6

Assess and Project
Conduct a "fit-gap" to determine the plan of action

With the completion of the last chapter, we have begun our journey with a comprehensive determination of our current situation. Similar to the process we utilize when driving an automobile, we consult a roadmap to navigate our vehicle and its contents to the destination in the shortest possible distance. While the roadmap does not "tell" us the safest or most efficient routes, it provides us information to make an informed decision. In the previous chapter, we created the roadmap of our current state or "As-Is" condition. At this point, we should clearly understand our circumstances, our strengths, weakness, and opportunities that confront our profits, personnel, and customers.

This chapter concentrates on defining the roadmap to migrate our organization from its "As-Is" state to a future position (*i.e.,* a "To-Be" standing). The "To-Be" environment is the logical point in the future that the organization wishes to achieve. Utilizing this future position, organizational goals, objectives and measurements can be reached. The "To-Be" environment can only be obtained by discerning and predicting the future industry, business, organizational, and technology drivers that will be acting upon the corporation. The "To-Be" status provides the end-point for innovative relevance. However, the "To-Be" state also reacts to changes within the drivers, thereby providing a methodical and focused evolution of the realignment processes. Since the "To-Be" position is an ever-moving window of achievement and success, the process embedded in this chapter provides the "ever-greening" stimulus, which is required for innovative relevance realignment of the organization (see *Figure 6.1*).

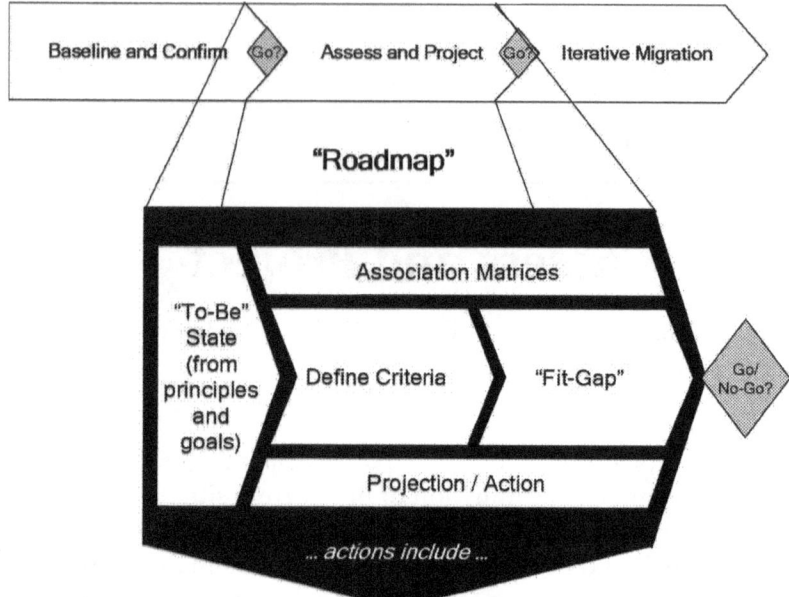

Figure 6.1—Access and Project Segmentation

This roadmap definition provides us with a set of boundaries from which to delineate an effective realignment strategy with defensible action plans. Realignment projection, once the "fit-gap" has been completed, is analogous to discerning where you are on the roadmap. It is a determination of whether your "vehicle" is capable of making the journey given the time, resources, and sacrifices, which must be performed to reach the destination. This projection provides a secondary check to determine if the end positioning is too aggressive for the organization's maturity or culture. If the plan extends the organization too far beyond its abilities, then the action plans and realignment efforts will result in further deterioration and ineffectiveness.

Define the "To-Be" state

Definition of the future or "To-Be" position is many times fraught with peril for internal teams attempting to utilize innovative relevance. The self-preservation inherent in our human condition, significantly limits our ability to forecast programs, which could adversely affect our status or employment condition. To further complicate the situation, we are continuously presented with "best practices" and industry "normalized" models by technocrats, venture capitalists, financial investors, board members, peers, customers, and alliances—all possessing "the answer." Consequently, the "To-Be" situation can sometimes, if not properly framed, represent an unattainable and expensive model that threatens to bankrupt the organization and alienate the customer base.

If we review what we've already discussed in Chapter 1, we have created and adopted a set of principles needed to guide our organization forward. These principles can then be integrated with:

Goals: Defines the "what we are going to achieve?" Framed by the principles, these three to eight action items articulate definitive achievements being sought by the enterprise within the next 0 to 36 months.

Objectives: Measurable and quantifiable accomplishments that are segmented by division. There are typically two to three objectives for each goal. Each objective can span a period of 0 to 18 months. They are refreshed and adjusted quarterly, as necessitated to account for results and feedback.

Policies: Support the three critical components of the "To-Be" situation—Principles, Goals, and Objectives. Polices can be decomposed in later stages into procedures and schedules, which have discrete measurements for inclusion into sustaining systems, dashboards, business intelligence efforts, and statistical analysis.

Processes: With the framework in place, enterprise and secondary processes can be defined and adopted. These processes are developed to address the realization mechanics required for the iterative migration steps, which will be defined in Chapter 7. They support the defined hierarchy of needs as identified from the vision, assessment, and projection.

The "To-Be' framework provides the filtering mechanism to determine investment relevance and required innovation needed to achieve the realignment programs (see *Figure 6.2*).

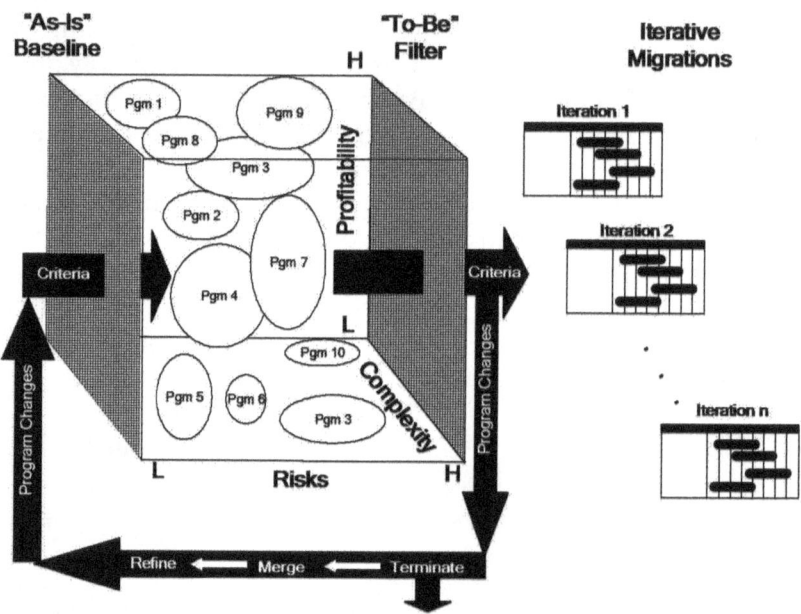

Figure 6.2—"To-Be" acts like a "Filter"

Creation of this future state requires careful consideration and painstaking adherence to the guiding principles. At the end of this step, it is recommended that confirmation of the "To-Be" components be finalized with the realignment's sponsors. Stakeholder's directions, biases, and confirmation needs should be addressed under the guidance of the realignment sponsors.

The delivery of the future framework is not typically about the "how" of achievement, as these questions are left to the program particulars and plans. For instance, the use of web services, data warehousing, and dashboards, provide needed insight into customer buying habits for particular brands. These components are elements framed within the programs, which help the organization achieve a given profitability level. They are just the means of getting us to our real goal of "an increase of 25% improvement in per customer profitability due to more efficient cross-selling of vertical product lines."

Associate the states

For an accurate projection, the artifacts from the baseline need to be aligned with the projections of the "To-Be" modality. This association is best achieved using a series of integrated association matrices or cubes. These multidimensional models provide the realignment leader and team a method to ask the difficult questions (as illustrated below) and forecast anticipated actions.

- How will our prior investments in technology support the need for greater profitability per customer?

- Will increased brand differentiation result in a lower cost of inventory with higher turnover rates? Where do we invest to achieve the returns within seven months?

- What level of staffing is sufficient to meet a 25% increase in customer calling, 15% increase in sales, and a 22% decrease in call backs due to improved "house holding" penetration?

- To improve our servicing profitability with our recent acquisition, what investments need to be made to deliver volumes by 5-, 10-, and 20-fold to capitalize on shifting customer demographics due to delinquencies, abandonments, and foreclosures?

- With workforce globalization, what effect would a 15% shift of domestic resources to offshore outsourcers have on the customer and brand perceptions? Purchasing habits?

- If we increased personnel education by 35% to leverage our $14.3 million investment in collaborative software and web services, can we offset this cost differential with faster time to market, reduced turnover, improved profitability, higher quality, and less rework?

The affiliation of artifacts requires experience. They will need to be categorized not only into their baseline alignments, but this then needs to be segmented into the "To-Be" categories for applicability (see *Figure 6.3*).

The use of technology in this segment is recommended, but not mandatory. The sophistication can range from simple spreadsheets indexed to filing cabinets to data cubes utilizing knowledge and compliance software. If the realignment team is inexperienced, it is suggested that you choose the basics and shy away from complex processes, hardware, or software to track, integrate, and determine migration programs. Too often, innovative relevance teams become guilty of applying irrelevant solutions as the means become the end-state. For experienced teams and leaders, the use of high-value solutions to assist with diagnosis, collaboration, registration, publication, and confirmation are invaluable and cost-effective.

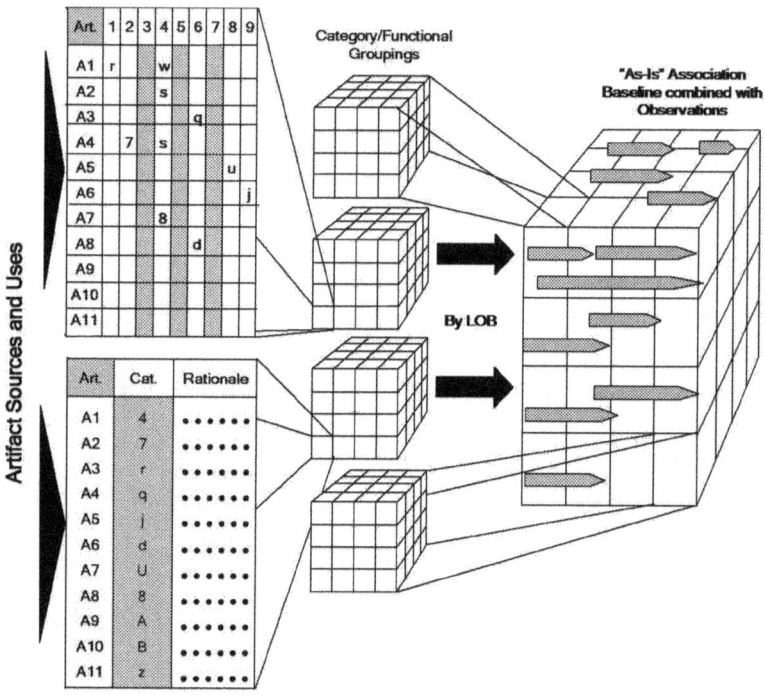

Figure 6.3—Artifact Associations

The baseline measurements provide the realignment effort critical metrics to determine the number and frequency of iterations, which must take place for the programs to achieve their end-state. In many cases, an organization cannot leap from a tier four to a tier one company in a single sequence. It requires several steps and on-going adjustment depending upon the results of the prior programs. It is commonly referred to as "think big—start small." The correct association of the measurements provides the objective foundation for determining how aggressive you can be with the realignment programs.

Define the criteria

Criteria for success are derived from the goals, objectives, and principles defined within the "To-Be" model. Criteria need to be mapped to the baseline assessments and measurements taken previously. In utilizing the prior measures, along with additional criteria for improvements, a comprehensive set of integrated and quantitative metrics can be used to track progress. The metrics provide a foundation for the objective evaluation of the approaches employed within the iterative migration programs. These criteria can be thought of as milestones of progression rather than as substitutes for the larger goals, objectives, and principles previously established.

Moreover, if we examined our own organizations, we would probably uncover several thousand basic measurements. These measurements are usually examined for financial profitability, expense management, capital expenditures, system availability, product sales, output produced, and other operational categories. However, if these operational measurements and their processes were examined from a macro business perspective, it would be apparent that they are often unrelated, reactionary, inconsistent, or monitor only a discrete portion of the sub-process. These measures lack cause and effect relationships, and they do not prompt immediate corrective action before "we hit the wall." For a realignment effort, our measurement criteria must be relevant for our innovative solutions. Experience, organizational culture, risk, aggressiveness, and complexity of the realignment effort will greatly influence the selection criteria and compelling measures.

The creation of the criteria starts with:

- What are the targeted and approved organizational goals and objectives?

- What has the success rate been for the achievement of current and prior goals and objectives (operational or strategic)?

- How do you measure these results?

- Are there clearly defined milestones and/or deliverables?

- What are the risks and how do you measure and monitor these?

- Does the organizational culture understand and accept these measures?

- Are we using manual or automated processes to capture measurements?

- What measures are critical to success and how do they relate to the end-results?

- Is the measuring process on-time for decision making timeframe requirements?

By utilizing these foundational questions to determine appropriate criteria for success, those methods and techniques that are unfocused and ill-defined can be eliminated from the process before the effort is expended (to capture and report on their progress).

Conduct a "fit-gap" analysis

With the criteria understood, the baseline completed, and the "To-Be" model defined, we need to chart a set of programs and activities to make the future realignment requirements tangible. Although, before we can fund the programs and assign the resources, we need to understand how large and complex of a realignment program we are proposing.

We create this comprehension using a "fit-gap" analysis. From a macro view, we use our associations to determine where the "gaps" in delivery, process, resources, organization, and technology reside between the "As-Is" (baseline) and the "To-Be" model. We then "fit" a sequence of steps and actions to help us meet the criteria (driven by the "To-Be" model) to reveal the most effective and practical migration approach. Innovative realignment "fit-gap" analysis once defined will need to be examined for duplications and synergies between criteria, achievement goals, and objectives. Additionally, critical assumptions and key success factors will need to be documented to ensure that as the business and program environments evolve, the underlying activity sequences have necessary transparency to the map the deviations.

To aid with realignment fit-gap, I have developed a deficiency assessment model shown in its macro status (see *Figure 6.4*). This model describes the problems that can be exacerbated by realignment efforts too far reaching for the organization's planning, operating principles, processes, controls and communication capabilities. The model was developed to demonstrate that the lack of business fundamentals (see shaded areas) significantly contributes to fragmented solutions, organizational dysfunctionality, and unrealized profits. Conversely, the model can also be used to show the positive benefits of providing business leadership and organizational consistency. These relationships provide valuable insight into innovative relevance issues which must be solved before realignment migration can be effective and sustainable.

Figure 6.4—Organizational Deficiencies

When examining the information flows between the relationships, it becomes obvious that Planning and Principle Philosophy, as well as Process, Controls, and Communication significantly affect the other functional areas. In fact, failure to solve problems in these two (2) functional areas cause 70% of the problems typically attributed to downstream realignment programs (see *Figure 6.5*). The ability to create additional corporate value using innovative relevance resides not with just the technology or process, but with its integration into the organization, its architecture, and its cultural acceptance.

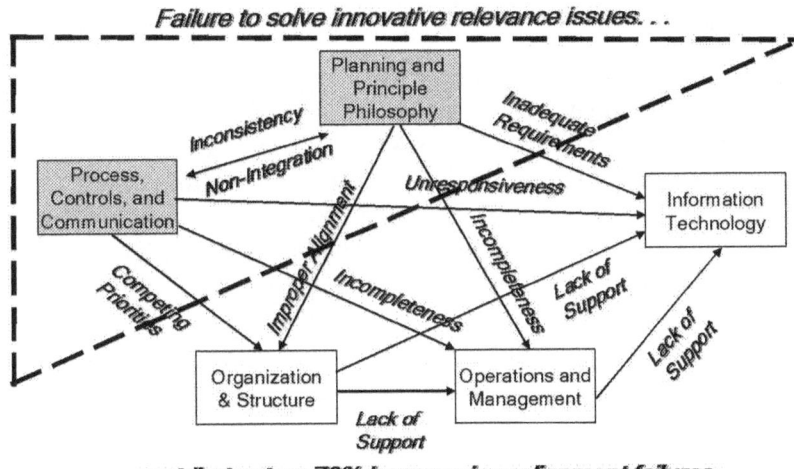

Figure 6.5—Deficiencies Contribution Significance

It provides the initial foundation for review and assessment while position-ing solutions for realignment programs. Addressing the deficiencies creates positive solution relationships (see *Figure 6.6*).

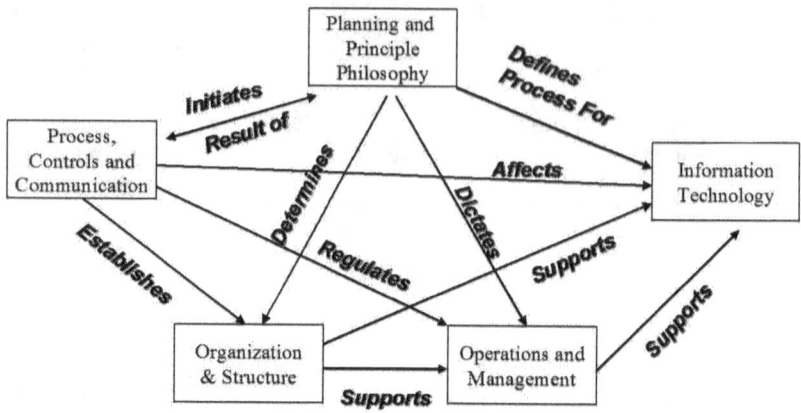

Figure 6.6—Mitigating Deficiencies Creates Momentum

Using the macro models as architecture for the fit-gap" activities, detailed sequences can be determined (see *Figure 6.7*). With the sequences identified, the projection of the action plans can be undertaken. The compilation of these sequences, form the targeted programs that will need to be sourced, loaded, and funded.

Define the action plans—project forward

With the definition of the realignment complete, a practical set of migra-tion plans can be created. The development of the migration plans allows the organization to clearly define what is to be accomplished, where they are to start, how to achieve the desired results, and the milestones used to bench-mark the innovative relevance process. These plans will include a prioritized schedule of business and technology projects, driven by the "roadmap" in the prior stages. This stage will identify specific action steps, skills, and technolo-gies required to successfully complete the realignment. In addition, the migration projects will include the required resources, the organizational structure, and the associated risks. The projection utilizes the fit-gap results to determine the best framework or structure for the "To-Be" state of the organi-zation's investments.

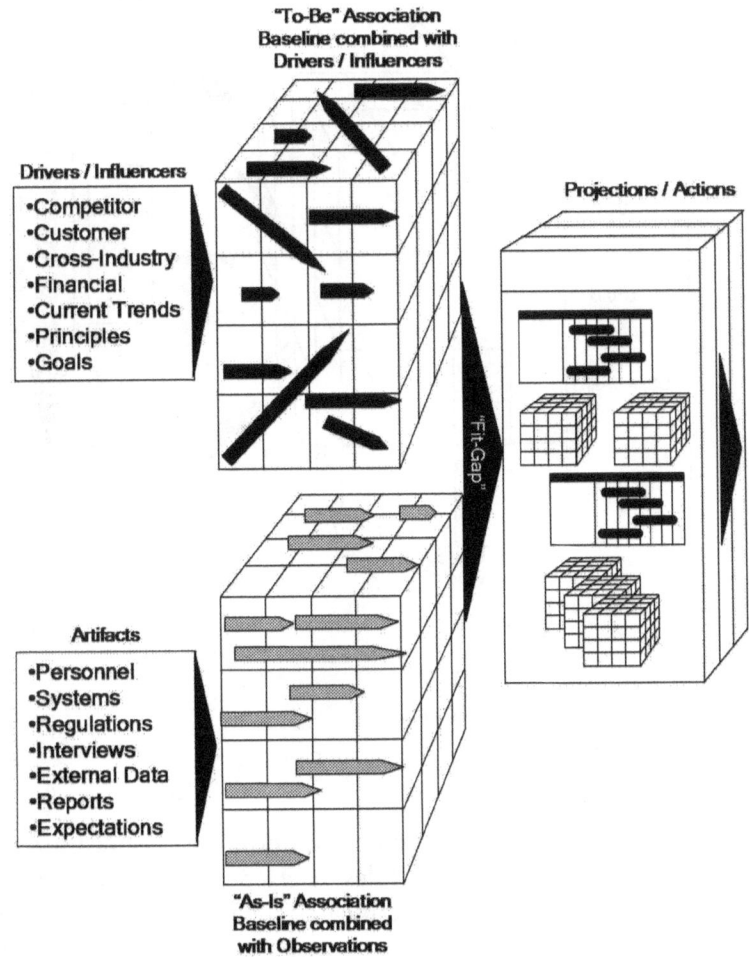

Figure 6.7—Determination of Detailed "Fit-Gap" Sequences

In defining the action plans (see *Figure 6.8*), organizational constraints identified in the assessment can be utilized to create a pragmatic and achievable approach. As we've already detailed, failure to utilize these constraints will result in an approach that may be excellent, but cannot be implemented with the required quality, timing, and personnel.

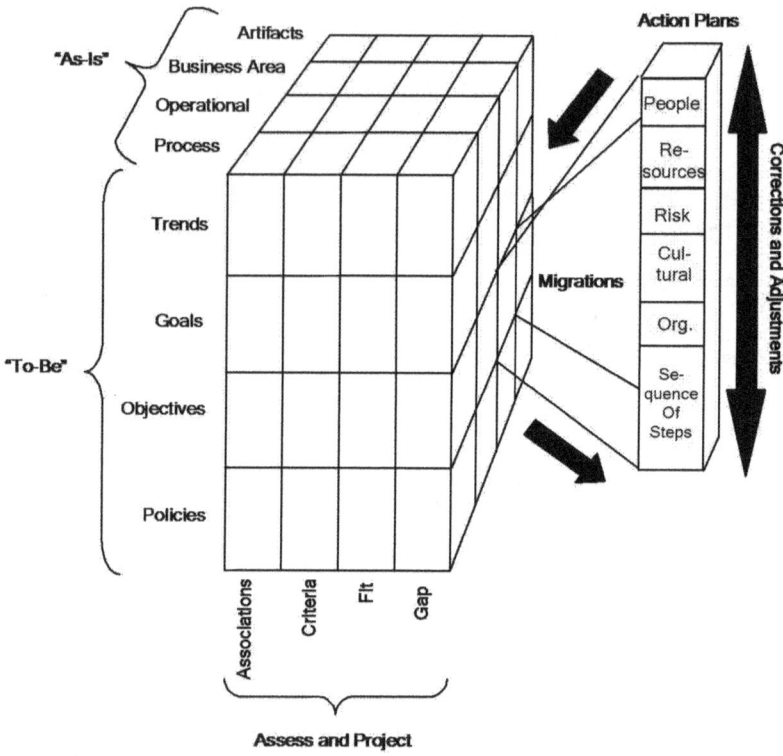

Figure 6.8—Projecting Forward

An effective series of action plans will build upon the organization's set of directions, goals, objectives, and principles. The approach must definitively support the business processes that are critical to the achievement of the organization's strategic objectives. This strategy integration is critical to the articulation of the organizational initiatives into principles, directions, and standards.

Go/No-Go?

Just as we concluded the baselining effort with decisions for continuance, the Assess and Project stage also requires an active confirmation process. The "Go/No-Go" confirmation activities in this stage are even more critical than the prior meetings with the sponsors and stakeholders. For at the end of this process sequence, we will need significant, continuous commitment and visibility from the organization.

This chapter has defined the actions and events that must take place for the organization to achieve its "To-Be" status. The monies, resources, and commitments demanded for realignment cannot be taken lightly. As we'll see in the next chapter, the organization will need to migrate towards the discrete objectives one step at a time. We cannot hope to launch all actions at once or achieve complex interdependent processes, when our corporation and its culture are operating at a rudimentary delivery level. It will take iterative migration steps combined with accurate tracking, expectation management, and humility.

Lessons learned

Innovative relevance requires a clearly defined roadmap to move the organization from a current location to a forecasted destination. The "itinerary" to reach the projected location requires definition of the goals and objectives needed to identify the positional criteria for success.

The achievement of a "To-Be" projection is just as much about the journey of stepwise obtainment as it is meeting the profit goals.

- Goal and objective integration is mandated to provide the foundation for subsequent criteria segmentation and definition.

- Success criteria must support the realignment's vision, principles, goals, and objectives to ensure that these granular measures impart the necessary guidance and checkpoints required by the initiative teams.

- Comprehensive processes and policies are used to assess the efficacy of the current results and projections for the future state.

- The "To-Be" state must be driven by competitor, customer, cross-industry, financial, and current trends, while adhering to pre-established principles, goals, and objectives.

- The associative nature of the realignment states requires experience using multi-dimensional analysis techniques.

- Sourcing and uses of artifact complexity is reduced with the design and deployment of an End-to-End Informational Management repository (see Chapter 11).

- At the end of the baseline and assessment efforts, a confirmation from the sponsors and critical stakeholders must be obtained before additional investments are allocated or resources assigned to the innovative relevance initiatives.

- The "fit-gap" analysis not only requires suitable deployment of methods and techniques to achieve sourcing effectiveness, but prior experience with establishing linkages, causes and effects, and determination of action sequences.

Chapter 7

Iterative Migration

Begin the journey one step at a time

Congratulations! You have now created your roadmap and the sequence of steps needed to get you and the organization from your current condition ("As-Is") to the projected position ("To-Be"). The obtainment of innovative relevance now rests with the execution and adjustment of the programs defined within the Assess and Project stage. These architectonic programs represent the commencement of transformation. Realignment programs provide the mechanics for sustainability and provide the organization with a means for tracking progress and adjusting proposed activities.

With the definition of the realignment roadmap complete, a practical set of migration activities can be substantiated. The development of the migration plans allows the organization to clearly identify what is to be accomplished, where they are to start, how to achieve the desired results, and the milestones used to benchmark the realignment process. Migration plans will include a prioritized schedule of business and technology projects (as part of larger programs), which were determined during the development of the "roadmap" and supporting criteria. In addition, the migration projects will include the required resources, the organizational structure, the associated risks, and mitigation strategies (see *Figure 7.1*).

Migration is seldom achievable in one step or sequence of activities. It will take numerous programs and supporting projects to accomplish a viable realignment culture, profits, and delivery environment. By utilizing an iterative approach where the programs are required to achieve measurable and definitive qualitative and quantitative criteria, effective adjustments can be made "just-in-time" to minimize waste and rework. Active and frequent measurements are mandated with this approach promoting exacting and integrated controls—which are viewed positively in innovative realignment initiatives.

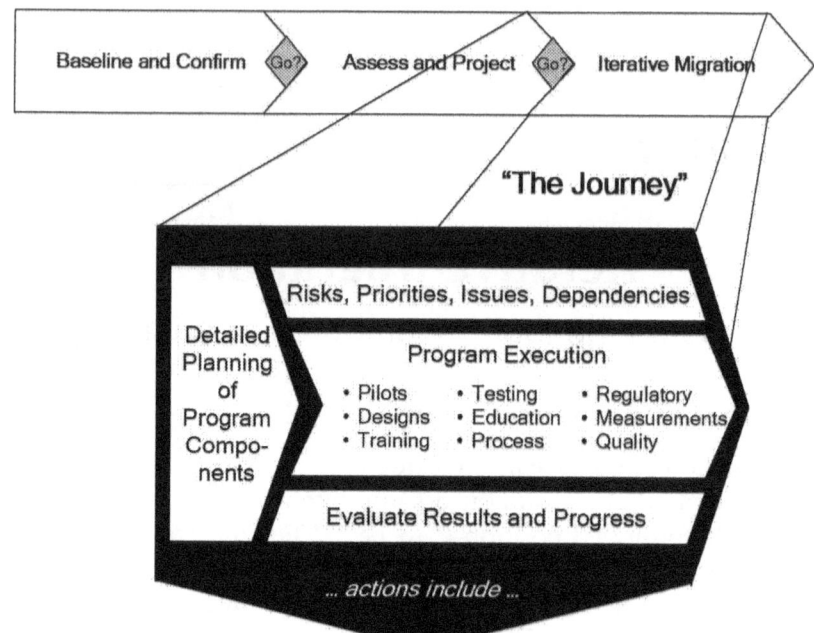

Figure 7.1—Iterative Migration

The migration stage identifies the interrelationships, risks, and costs of the defined realignment process at discrete, compartmentalized programs and supporting projects. Iterative delivery creates an incremental blueprint required to make the theoretical projected positioning a reality. Iterative migration is defined as the:

Derivation of activities and priorities required to realign an organization from their "As-Is" status of operations to a "To-Be" position. It utilizes the baselining, assessment, and projection results to create an integrated set of programs, plans, and priorities.

To take advantage of iterative techniques, programs should be kept under 120 days in duration (target is 90 days). This timeframe allows for quick "mid-course corrections" using experiential data to update the plans, priorities, and risks.

Detailed planning

Within today's business climates, the creation of detailed plans for programs and projects is extensively documented and discussed. There are numerous techniques, software programs, certifications, and case-studies on successes and failures. Even within your own organization, there may be multiple thought disciplines surrounding the appropriate level of detail needed to manage programs and projects. We will address the critical components required for minimal program management.

Purpose/Scope: Succinctly stated, "What is the program trying to accomplish?" Hard-hitting and factual, it should describe the intent, business area impact, and general goals to be accomplished. For added clarity, objective, associative mapping should be utilized.

In-Scope/Out-of-Scope: While the previous element defined the macro level of accomplishment, this next level will specifically highlight what will be covered and what is excluded from consideration. This area is often times segmented further using sub-classifications of business area, location/division, process, data usage, regulatory, and information technology.

Deliverables/Milestones: Within the scope of the program, definitive accomplishments will aid with the obtainment of the end goals and objectives. These deliverables articulate the logical measurements that provide realignment success. Significant deliverables are obtained usually every 30 days or less.

Roles/Responsibilities: Programs require people, departments, or service providers to perform a sequence of steps necessary to achieve the deliverables and overall program scope of work. As such, all involved parties need to understand their responsibilities, required timings, and functional roles with the program.

Management Processes: Widely documented and discussed, programs require processes and procedures on how to consistently define, communicate, track, and report on cross organizational a) issues, b) changes, c) finances, and d) statuses. Use of "red, yellow, green" (RYG) is a popular method to track projects that are to be rolled-up underneath a larger program.

Budgets: Standardized formats, processes, and procedures are mandatory. Technology standardization in this area is recommended to avoid consolidation (*i.e.*, roll-up) disparity and granularity issues.

Plans: Countless books and training courses are available on this subject. The definitions of project plans are aided by vendor solutions, methodologies, prescriptive templates, and cross-domain successes and failures. Plans should be segmented into phases, activities, and tasks. Tasks should not contain any more than 40 hours of cumulative time. Tasks are logically grouped into common activities, which in turn are assembled to form program phases or stages.

Assumptions, Factors, Criteria: All assumptions, success factors, and prerequisite criteria need to be defined and documented, so that as the efforts progress they can be either validated or adjusted. Adjustments in these areas can have a material effect on the overall success and program approach utilized by the team. Additionally, as they are compiled, cross-functional program alignments can be assembled to determine adjustments to plans, budgets, deliverables, and scope.

Experience demands a strong word of caution for leaders hoping to delegate this responsibility—beware! Project planning is not program management. Certifications for large program management (*i.e.*, > $15 million USD) needed for innovative realignments do not exist. Less than 1% of project managers make realignment program managers needed for your team, and its long-term success. Program leaders adhere to the qualities of financial acumen, cross-domain knowledge, operational leadership, and IT knowledge (for an extensive explanation, see Chapter 3). It is only with proven results and delivery experiences provided by the program leaders, that accurate and detailed planning can be accomplished. This requirement is created by the need for the deployment of iterative migration program techniques, which provide the corporation with a technique to cope with rapidly changing organizational demands.

Risks, priorities, issues, and dependencies

With the programs granularly defined and communicated, realignment efforts can now concentrate on the projected interdependencies, issues, assumptions, and required returns. However, as a result of limited resources, competing schedules, and constraining budgets, the prioritization of programs must be objectively determined.

Therefore, a necessary action within the iterative migration stage is to identify the interrelationships, risks, and returns for each realignment program (see *Figure 7.2*). This step accepts input from the detailed planning process and assists with the determination of pre-execution allocations, commitments, cross-functional relationships, and business-driven priorities.

Innovative relevance requires making choices. These choices include investments, training, education, processes, and personnel, to name just a few. For these reasons, the dynamics between the realignment programs must be carefully analyzed for duplication, inefficiencies, competing demands, and excessive program aggressiveness. Using a "Prioritization Cube" to assist with the sequencing and assignments can greatly improve the compartmentalization and reusability of results, while maximizing the expended effort of the organization and its participants.

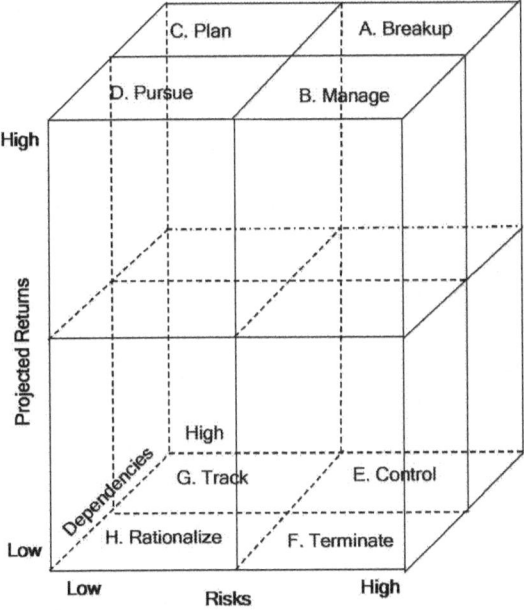

Figure 7.2—The Prioritization Cube

Programs that fall within the eight quadrants should be examined by the realignment team to further refine or adjust its plans and activities. Adjustments, based upon the risk classifications, provide the initiative's focused insight to manage expectations, improve probability of success, and balance the triple constraints of program management.

A. **Breakup**: Programs that exhibit these characteristics should be decomposed into more discrete elements. The ability to manage the complex interdependencies, benefits, and risks cannot be achieved within a common effort. Breaking the program up allows for improved performance, communications, and results.

B. **Manage**: High risk, high return programs need to be tightly managed with substantive risk mitigation techniques and plans. These programs are not inherently "bad," but they should be approached with caution, and implemented under stringent procedures and controls.

C. **Plan**: High return, low risk efforts with extensive dependencies require rigorous planning and program controls. Use of time tracking, issue management, statistical analysis of results, and program office techniques must be employed.

D. **Pursue**: Programs in this quadrant should be aggressively pursued. The high return, low risk with minimal dependent programs can yield significant short-term results to sustain and further the obtainment of organizational realignment goals.

E. **Control**: Initiatives in this quadrant are usually required to support higher return programs. As such, these efforts need to be approached using extraordinary measurements, peer reviews, and delivery validations to ensure risk mitigations and promotion of scope restraints.

F. **Terminate**: Programs that are deemed to have a high risks, low benefits, and low interdependencies, may be candidates for termination. These programs need to be reviewed by the realignment team to either redefine the effort, or collapsed it into a more significant endeavor where the risks are not as pronounced.

G. **Track**: With low risk, minimal return, and high dependencies, these quadrant assessed programs will need to be tracked to promote delivery. Their potential impact on related efforts is demanding their successful completion.

H. Rationalize: Programs in this area must be reexamined for applicability to the realignment efforts. There will be valuable programs in this area, but they may not have a high degree of tangible returns. They should be rationalized, and if confirmed, they should be allowed to proceed.

The prioritization of programs should not be undertaken without due consideration. Using a methodical and prescriptive approach can allow the team to avoid committing resources and monies to efforts that have marginal values. However, the application of the prioritization matrix should not be used like a "cookbook." Experience and situational events will have a marked influence on prioritization, material issues, and cross-domain dependencies.

An example of programs applied to the matrix is shown in *Figure 7.3*. Just like your situation, not all programs will fit neatly into each quadrant. Some initiatives will overlap due to timings, durations, variabilities, and experiential data judgments of the realignment team. As we can see, programs 1, 4, and 5 falls within our "pursue" classification. Program 8 has shown it has a large degree of variability, and will be a program requiring significant management oversight and operational review. Program 2 is a candidate for reexamination as it pervades too many quadrants—may be the result of intermixed goals, deficient plans, disjointed deliverables, or all the above.

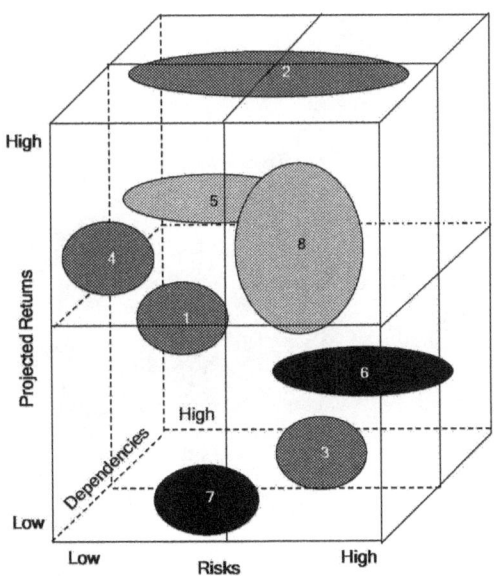

Figure 7.3—Example Prioritization Cube[xxii]

Moreover, the use of the prioritization cube must be employed for individual program iterations executed within the realignment's framework. The cube's usage is part of the innovative relevance process. It should be implemented to guarantee appropriate program classification, appreciation of risks, and expectation management realization.

Program execution

A tremendous amount of work and intellectual capital have been expended by you, the organization, and your realignment team. At this point, the programs are defined, the plans are detailed, and the priorities and interrelationships are set and understood. The excitement should be high, and the commitment and clamoring for realignment success deafening. You and your team should be commended!

We're now ready to act upon those commitments, promises, and expectations made by your teams, sponsors, and stakeholders. Program execution involves a great many variables some of which are outside of your control (but should have been identified with mitigation solutions in your risk analysis). Our journey and the organizational profits are now in your hands. Twenty years ago, I received advice from a mentor on my first realignment effort that still rings true today—"Hang on; it's going to be an intense ride…"

The fundamentals of program execution should entail:

Kick-off: Communicate the goals, objectives, processes, and expectations to the team. Distribute the detailed plans and obtain commitment from each person on their schedules and responsibilities.

Training: Conduct all initial training to promote awareness, adherence to standards, and correct procedural usage.

Designs: Delineate the designs, scenarios, and implementation approaches needed to obtain the solutions outlined within the program.

Pilots: Where appropriate, use the designs within a pilot situation to validate the approaches. Pilots are practical steps which can eliminate unnecessary expenditures, cost overruns, and flawed designs from affecting downstream actions and phases. Pilots help capture the specifics of the "solution theory" before enterprise roll-out.

Process: The redesigns of processes are concurrently executed with the inclusive projections and activities of the program. Process redesign or establishment should adhere to standards promoted using BPM[xxiii], application process exchange (APEX), BPO[xxiv], or Six Sigma.

Regulatory: With an average of 15% compounded yearly increase[xxv] in regulatory oversight, the integration of critical and anticipated compliance requirements must be included as part of the design and process determinations (see Chapter 13).

Measurements: Are used to capture on-going metrics for improvements, results, and corrections that can be integrated with a continuous improvement process. Measurements will support industry techniques, enterprise quality, and globalization efforts.

Quality: Our delivery of services and products must realize that profitability resides with the purchasing customer. Therefore, we must make certain substantial consideration is given to meet or exceed quality standards, procedures, and methods. Delivery frameworks, such as ISO 9000, Six Sigma, and lean manufacturing, must be followed to promote quality integration with the program's goals.

Education: When the design is confirmed and the pilots are complete, the program should be preparing for the enterprise's education. This education can involve new alliances, policies, informational usage, brands, customer segmentation, or financial requirements. Education must be undertaken to promote sustainability and conformance.

Testing: When the program has internally met its requirements, methods, and techniques necessary to achieve or exceed its stated scope, it must be tested to ensure confidence in the projected results. These confirmed results will serve as the foundation for the realignment activities' subsequent baselines, warranted by the use of iterative migration methods (that will follow the program's successful deployment).

The integration of the program's execution steps, can be significantly augmented with off-the-shelf methodologies and existing internal, enterprise-wide programs. It should be noted, that not all of the segments listed above, may apply to each and every one proposed realignment programs. It will take experienced program leaders to determine the appropriate sequences and execution coverage's necessary for the desired results.

Results and progress

The end result for realignment measurements is an electronic dashboard or portal, which utilizes primitive program metrics and related sources to create meaningful "gauges" of progress, goal obtainment, issue delineation, and statistical significance with "drill-up, drill-down" capabilities. The composition of the dashboard metrics starts with trained personnel who are executing the programs. It culminates with the integration of disparate sources to forecast and predict results, which merge to form management and operational indicators. These indicators are used to make adjustments in allocations, scope, timelines, and interdependencies, while dealing with problems or changes in assumptions and risks.

The creation of a dashboard is dependent upon the complexity, duration, and realignment scope at the nucleus of the innovative relevance programs. In *Figure 7.4*, a conceptual dashboard of tracking and controls are integrated to form a cohesive set of metrics that can then be used to deduce and forecast events.

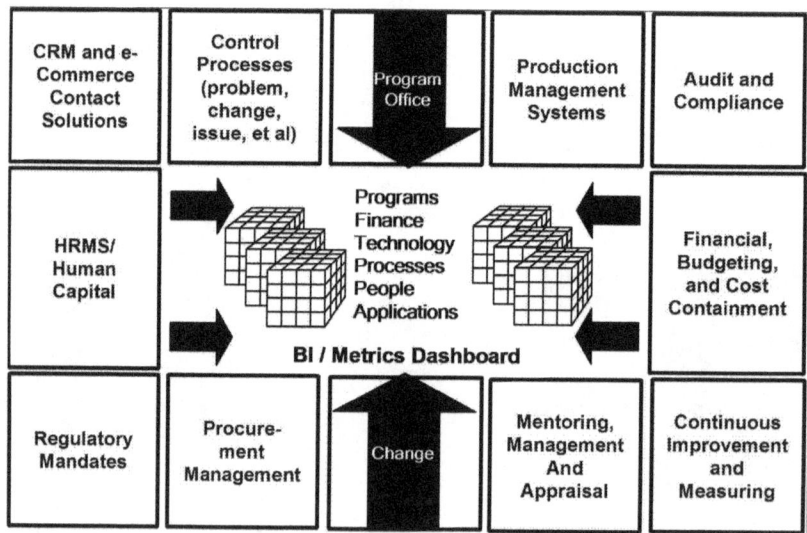

Figure 7.4—Illustrative Dashboard Sources

The sophistication of the dashboard can be accomplished using desktop PC tools, but their true value can only be realized using more advanced, predictive methods and techniques. Dashboards and portals can be very effective when the enterprise is already culturally conditioned to regimented processes and technologies including; business intelligence, cube analytics, multivariate, and statistical analysis.

Metric reporting must be disciplined and consistent from period to period to ensure accurate projections and statistical relevance. Failure to adhere to basic informational gathering processes and techniques of program management will result in "driving with your eyes closed." The metric gathering and reporting provides a concrete and measurable method to track programs which involve global resources, dependent priorities, cultural resistance, and complex execution.

The benefits of focused and results-oriented dashboards are unique to the organization in which they are deployed and internalized. Nevertheless, there are common advantages that are realized from the deployment of a program-driven dashboard or portal:

- Faster information delivery to decision making personnel,

- Compels proactive problem notification before they are released to the customer base,

- Promotes focus on the core or critical indicators,

- Improves analysis while promoting accurate decision making,

- Reduces manual integration and dissemination efforts,

- Facilitates integrated vertical operational measures, and

- Monitors trends and forecasts the potential outcome.

By using synthesized methods and techniques, organizations can begin to have a proactive influence on their business processes and realignment results. Distinct and repeatable measurements provide the benefits of managing the deluge of information received from dispersed programs into a manageable subset, which can be utilized for the organization's actions and corrections. The timeliness and accuracy of data is too often underestimated. The failure to address data quality issues and delivery (*i.e.*, sourcing) constraints will result in lost opportunities, cost overruns, and wasted efforts.

Lessons learned

Just as we travel in an automobile or plane, we need to make the journey a mile at a time. The realization of our destiny cannot be achieved with science fiction "teleportation" techniques. Therefore, we need to structure programs in segments or iterations, which can be completed in compartmentalized durations to ensure organizational sustainability.

- Use of predefined program management techniques and procedures is mandatory.

- Training and education for participants is required in advance of meaningful actions within the programs.

- Detailed planning and priorities must be defined using objective analysis and classifications.

- The adoption of a prioritization cube for decision making can lend consistency and efficacy to resource loadings, program investments, and operating risks.

- Regardless of the industry models used for program execution, clear roles, responsibilities, and deliverables must be defined with unambiguous accountabilities.

- Program integration for resources, assumptions, dependencies, issues, and scope adjustments must be established.

- Iterative steps will be required by programs, motivated by actual results and organizational feedback. Consequently, initiatives must be segmented into discernable steps with corrective action milestones contained in the program plans (*i.e.*, Go/No-Go).

SECTION 3

ANALYZE YOUR PROGRESS—
PREPARE FOR CHANGES

"Everyone thinks of changing the world, but no one thinks of changing themselves"

—Tolstoy

Decisions proliferate as you and the organization prepare to conduct realignment programs. This section tackles critical challenges presented to the innovative relevance teams as they confront the historical dogmas, arcane processes, and cultural resistance of realignment. We will apply Penrose's economic foundations to the selection and calculation of realignment alternatives concentrating on results and resources[xxvi].

The decisions and approaches within this section can have a profound affect not only on the programs' overall success, but market, brand, customer, alliance, and political perceptions outside of the immediate organizational boundaries. Innovative realignment decisions and programs are not insular—they have enterprise implications that will transcend the initiatives.

Chapter 8: Workforces—Making the Cuts

Chapter 9: Offshore, Onshore, Near Shore?

Chapter 10: Focusing on Returns

Chapter 11: Utilizing End-to-End Informational Management

Chapter 8

Workforces—Making the Cuts
Provide the incentives for change

In the last decade, staffing reductions were all about cost savings rather than improving profitability using innovative relevance. Often times, the real challenges for the realignment teams resided with the appropriate measurements and criteria for workforce adjustments and separations. Furthermore, if the team was composed of internal personnel, then the effect and first-hand knowledge of these reduction proposals along with their ramifications on morale, individuals, and their peers were immediately known—it became personal. The cutback or reassignment of personnel should never be taken lightly, or without careful planning to ascertain the conformance to objective rationale and subsequent implications of these workforce modifications.

Nevertheless, the realities of realignment programs are that assignments, roles, responsibilities, and organizational compositions will be different from the "As-Is" environment. It cannot be avoided or ignored. Realignments uncover high-value personnel who are not being utilized to their potential, while highlighting individuals that are not contributing to the organizational successes and profits in meaningful ways. The former individuals need to be strengthened and mentored, whereas the latter need to be examined for relevance within the organizational "To-Be" environment.

We will briefly examine five critical areas for assessing and projecting personnel (see *Figure 8.1*); 1) Skills assessments, 2) Performance mentoring, 3) Retraining and redeployment, 4) Reductions and eliminations, and finally 5) Outsourcing.

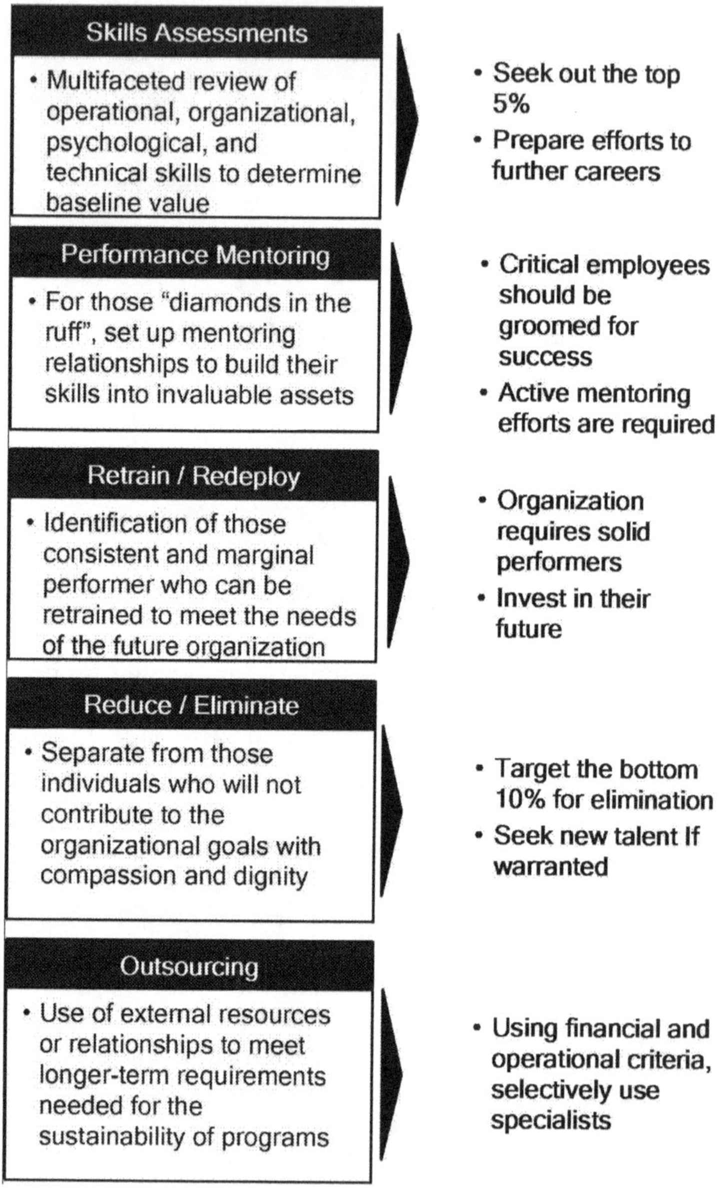

Skills Assessments

- Multifaceted review of operational, organizational, psychological, and technical skills to determine baseline value

- Seek out the top 5%
- Prepare efforts to further careers

Performance Mentoring

- For those "diamonds in the ruff", set up mentoring relationships to build their skills into invaluable assets

- Critical employees should be groomed for success
- Active mentoring efforts are required

Retrain / Redeploy

- Identification of those consistent and marginal performer who can be retrained to meet the needs of the future organization

- Organization requires solid performers
- Invest in their future

Reduce / Eliminate

- Separate from those individuals who will not contribute to the organizational goals with compassion and dignity

- Target the bottom 10% for elimination
- Seek new talent If warranted

Outsourcing

- Use of external resources or relationships to meet longer-term requirements needed for the sustainability of programs

- Using financial and operational criteria, selectively use specialists

Figure 8.1—Workforce Adjustment Approach

Skills assessment

The competitive, industry, and organizational drivers for innovative relevance are continuous and unrelenting. Therefore, the need for a dynamic and adaptable workforce in the face of incessant pressure is also an obligatory requirement if the organization has a chance to succeed in fiercely competitive global markets. People, and the skills they possess, are inextricably linked to organizational profits. As such, the selection, retention, and advancement of organizational performers are paramount to achieving meaningful results.

Within the programs defined, we will need varied skills to ensure they satisfy the roles, responsibilities, and requirements set forth. Sometimes, however, the people that are being recommended for the given roles do not meet the skill requirements. This can be a result of organizational politics, convenience, or availability. The objective approach for suitable personnel assignment and review resides with the creation of a skills set matrix.

The skills matrix provides an objective review based upon prior organizational performance, work history, education, and training. Your human resources (HR) department may have already compiled a list of critical skills for each employee as part of their continual education and performance review processes that take place yearly or quarterly. To fully utilize the excellent work accomplished by your HR group, you'll need to associate their processes and matrices contents against the realignment programs' criteria and requirements, which are driving the mandated program skills.

Once integrated and augmented by your own internal information and discovery efforts, you can now objectively assess the individual's value to your program. This assessment can be leveraged comprehensively across the realignment initiatives to ensure consistency and reusability, while reducing duplication of efforts.

Furthermore, the skills assessments and associations allow the executive sponsors to properly determine who the future critical performers will be when the organization has completed at least the first wave of iterative migrations (see *Figure 8.2*).

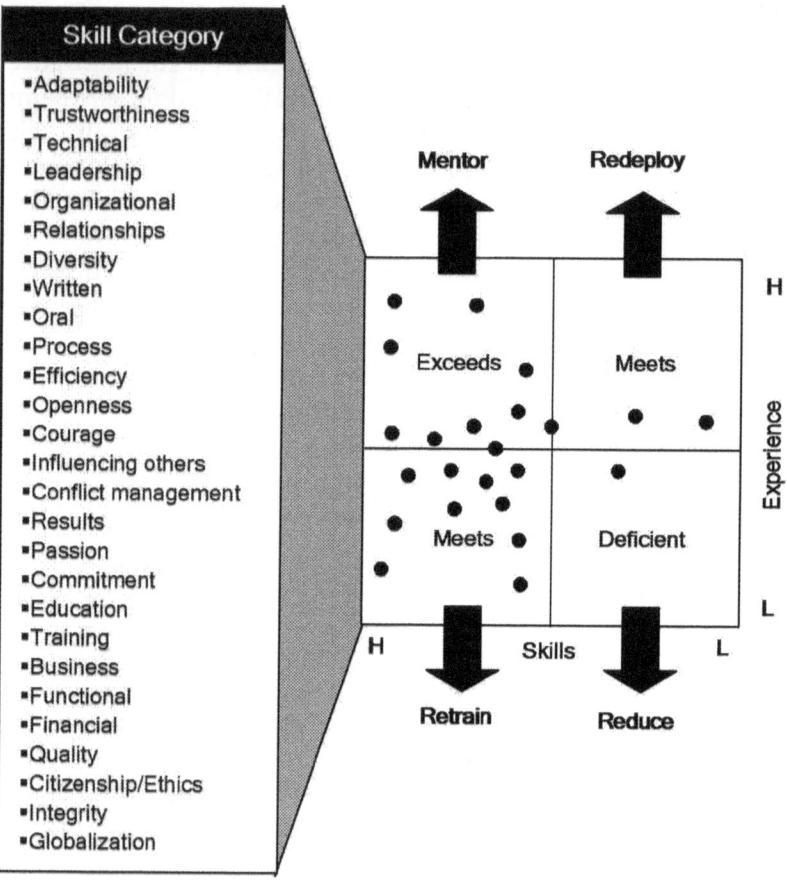

Figure 8.2—"Scatter" Assessment Technique

From the example assessment classifications shown in above figure, *a scatter diagram* of skills will be created using the matrix on the right-hand side of the graphic. These data points (created from the left-side) will need to be analyzed to determine the quadrant "collection" or set for a particular individual. Depending where the consensus resides, an aggregated and conclusive baseline will be created for the individual. This aggregation will assist with individual categorization for future action in the subsequent sections within this chapter.

Performance mentoring

With a definitive insight of your critical and future performers, the organization must provide the suitable incentives for individual nurturing and growth. For each individual who is selected to participate in this improvement effort, an appropriate coach must be assigned that provides the commitment, encouragement, confidence, involvement, and privacy demanded for positive results. Mentoring is not an overnight curriculum or a quick fix. It is an undertaking for long-term sustainability and profitability for the organization, shareholders, investors, and employees.

Mentoring is also not mutually exclusive from individual training and education, which may be required to promote the person's aspirations (while strengthening their skills). The mentor has a key obligation in this relationship. It is always in short supply, and often discounted—the investment of sufficient time. The mentor should expect between 8 to 16 hours per month to be invested in the individual being assigned to him or her. Mentoring failures are more often attributed to inferior time management, as compared to improper mentor to individual misalignment, weak performers, or lack of interest.

The selection of a correct mentor hinges on alignment of the individual's personal beliefs with those of the mentor. Alignment of a conflict-centric manager with those of a consensus building individual will have unpleasant results. The core values of the two must be in directional alignment rather than diametrically opposite directions. Failure to find the common ground and empathy will significantly discount the mentor's ability to positively influence the individual. The use of PI (Predictive Index) personality testing can be an excellent method to promote proper matching of mentors to high-performers. This testing approach is widely available, and most HR groups will have access to skilled, external subject matter experts who can administer the assessment.

While not widely practiced, mentoring should involve the establishment of a "contract" between the mentor and the individual. The contract outlines the commitments, roles, and responsibilities each is willing to put into the relationship. It will define schedules, timeframes, and milestones as appropriate to ensure each prepares in advance. Also, codes of conduct and integrity standards are outlined to promote assimilation into the baseline skills of the individual.

The "contractual" process starts with the pair discussing and answering goal oriented questions. These questions are unique to the organization, its industry, and the experience of the individual assigned to the mentoring program. Human resources (HR) should be actively consulted during this process (as throughout the complete performance mentoring procedure to ensure adherence to legal and organizational employment practices).

Employees who are having difficulty with a mentor and mentors who are "surprised" by their mentored individual should work with HR to create corrective courses of action. These relationships are constantly changing, so it is suggested that every three to six months a formalized review is conducted by HR of every mentoring relationship to document successes and preemptively diffuse problems. Realignment innovation is about consistency and sustainability to improve profits. Employees are the cornerstones, and an investment in the leaders, intellectual capitalists, and delivery personnel are mandated.

Retraining and redeployment

Those employees who are solid "B-C" performers should not be continually turned out unless they are no longer needed by the "To-Be" realignment. While this may run counter to some management gurus, the retention of existing employees can be a very beneficial and time-saving activity for the organization. This rationale stems from several factors.

First, the introduction of new individuals into critical realignment initiatives provides challenges for the programs by increasing its risk, organizational acceptance and dysfunctionality, and a lack of awareness of industry practices and requirements. While these objections can be moderated, realignment programs have a sense of urgency that can prohibit the incorporation of new members. This preclusion is due to the time required to ensure conformance to defined plans and objectives, while minimizing delivery disruptions and "stop-starts." If properly framed, the retraining of these solid performers can be highly cost effective by minimizing personnel changes. In addition, the retrained employee can be a "success story" that will continue to deliver long after the innovative relevance efforts have completed.

Improving the skill sets of experienced employees is traditionally the most straightforward of realignment tasks. Their experience with the corporation cultivates a foundation for comprehension and acceptance of the realignment drivers as defined in Chapter 1. These employees have invested significant amount of their careers with the organization, and can prove to be the most loyal of the staff. Independently, care must be taken not to retain those personnel who have demonstrated a continual proclivity for politics rather than results. An individual's organizational performance and experience must clearly show recurrent improvements, results, and acceptance of corporate transitions.

Training seminars should be included as part of an individual's improvement program, which requires the use of the employee for definitive realignment tasks and deliverables. The training costs (development and delivery) and dependencies must be incorporated into the detailed plans and budgets. The realignment directors and teams need to ensure that training is integrated across the programs to minimize redundancies, promote leveragabilities, and reduce scheduling conflicts.

The use of employee "retention" contracts is a practice that is gaining acceptance during innovative realignments. These binding documents set a predetermined period of time for those employees to remain with the corporation, once they have received training to meet their future job requirements. If they leave before the prescribed time (usually between 9 to 18 months), they are required to reimburse the corporation for the total training costs expended including their travel expenses. This type of contract greatly decreases those employees who are seeking to be reeducated on an organizational budget with intent to leave once the training is completed. When you consider that retraining investments can exceed many thousands of dollars per employee, this "guarantee" is a prudent idea with today's workforce and corporate cultures.

Redeployment may also require training and additional education. Additionally, redeployment is used for those experienced solid performers who have a solid skill base, but who may be lacking vertical disciplines needed for the "To-Be" programs. Inexperienced personnel are usually not redeployed due to the costs and inability to deal with unfamiliar organizational demands and requirements.

Reduction and elimination

Take little solace in this step, but it must be done. The methodical separation from the corporation of its marginal or underperformers needs to be straightforwardly and truthfully confronted. Realignment efforts are sometimes the catalyst that forces an organization to understand the need for new skills and varied experiences. Innovative programs depend on quality personnel. It requires those individuals who are passionate about realignment completion, and have the acumen needed to successfully conclude their assigned tasks.

Following a methodical and comprehensive review (*e.g.,* scatter assessment of skills), these individuals need to be identified. Once placed in this category, their ratings will require one final review for accuracy and extenuating circumstances. It is also a time for HR, corporate, and legal reviews to ensure conformity to local laws, employment contracts, state and federal guidelines. All preparations must be completed before an employee is notified of the forced separation.

Depending upon your organizational culture and the corporate ranking of the individual, there may be exit assistance that can be provided to make the separation less catastrophic for both parties.

Counseling: This service is used by many firms to reduce the personal impact to the employee. It can promote an assessment of their skills, career possibilities, educational assistance, and even professional openings. It is usually handled by an outside, contracted firm who specialized in this delicate and stressful service.

Outplacement: Usually reserved for senior managers, this service is allocated to an external firm who specializes in the needs and demands of experienced personnel. Outplacement firms have gained considerable attention with the staffing reductions of the last decade, but their costs can be prohibitive for smaller or medium sized firms.

University Partnerships: A new service has grown out of the bust of the "dotcoms" and market correction of 2000 to 2004. Federal, state, and local tax money has been allocated for the reeducation of the American worker. These services are offered at a nominal costs with additional assistance presented to aid the families of the displaced or terminated worker.

Severance: Common for corporate employees, this is a financial compensation (one-time or over a set period of time), which will be calculated and awarded based upon years of service and salary levels.

Retention Bonuses: Paid to those employees with unique skills that are needed for short-term actions, while the realignment is being concluded. Bonuses can range from the very simple to exceedingly complex depending upon the risk, length, and unique skill sets required.

The methods and techniques used to communicate with the employee should focus on how to help the individual move their life forward. It's not about promoting and justifying the realignment programs and projected organizational results. It's about having empathy. Separated employees will minimally need to understand what they are going to do about healthcare and benefits, what will the organization tell potential new employers, and what assistance will be made available to help them and their families.

Yes, it's a stressful time for everyone. However, with considerate planning and anticipation of individual needs, the separation efforts can be accomplished.

Outsourcing

Since 2000, this topic has invoked emotional exchanges that border on violence between the opposing activists. Globalization of efforts has been underway for more than a century. In fact, the concept of globalization and outsourcing permeates the cultures of civilized societies dating back to the Romans and Egyptians. Although in our new technologically knowledgeable society, the speed at which this can happen is often times, unprecedented.

Outsourcing for an organization, per the vendors, television, web, and radio advertising, is the "wave of the future", right? Outsourcing is a business decision and not an emotional one. For an organization, many detailed questions need to be asked and answered including:

1. What is the scope of the outsourcing arrangement?

2. Have we analyzed the use of selectively sourcing functions or embarking upon an "insourcing" solution to enrich our processes and procedures?

3. Are we approaching outsourcing for costs? Quality? Customer needs? Market pressures? Regulatory or legal complications?

4. Have we conducted our own baseline? What does our analysis point to as the options for improvements?

5. What lessons have the industry learned from prior contractual relationships? What are the caveats and benefits? What are the true numbers?

6. Can we hope to sustain the relationship with continual business pressures and changes? What will additions and adjustments cost the organization in time, money, and opportunity?

7. How can we ever regain the function once it has been outsourced?

8. What political, local, regulatory or governmental actions can we expect? What will this do for our brand, campaigns, and market perceptions?

We could fill pages with additional questions. A cause-effect analysis should be part of any outsourcing decision. Outsourcing is a case of "buyer-beware."

Even with adequate due diligence by both parties, the track record for successful and satisfied customers and providers has been mixed.

Business leaders with the G-7 have been embracing outsourcing for many decades. The cost savings and competitive advantages have proven considerable. The recipients of these relationships (*i.e.*, companies based in countries such as India, China, and the Philippines), have become wealthy and their employees are prospering. It is an arrangement that works, but not in every situation. Those organizations that outsource portions of their realignment efforts to outsourcers will introduce a new level of complexity and politics. Proceed with purpose, but recognize that outsourcing is not always the answer to address employee deficiencies or competitive gaps.

In the next chapter, we'll explore the contested topic of using offshore, onshore, or near shore resources and organizations to assist with innovative realignment programs and organizational goals.

Lessons learned

Depletion of qualified personnel has created significant challenges for the realignment leaders and their associated programs. To be successful, innovative relevance programs must examine their existing skill bases for retention, retraining, reeducation, and redeployment. Organizations must assess their fundamental ability to deal with transition, and "To-Be" personnel skills needed by the transformation initiatives. These include:

- Have we deployed a solution set that remedies our employees or contractors' lack of operational knowledge?

- The adage that "you live and die by day-to-day" still holds true. Do we have the correct people in place to keep your environment up and bulletproof?

- Was the aforementioned factored into the economic analysis of selecting and deploying the solution?

- How many professional services vendors do we have in-house today assisting your staff?

- Has the downturn in the technology market really brought us new and qualified personnel?

- Do we have the most cost effective and sustainable choices identified? What have we not considered or evaluated?

- Have we identified the sustainable skills needed in our new "To-Be" environment?

- Have we identified the people that will be assuming these critical voids and are they committed to our company for the long-term?

Chapter 9

Offshore, Onshore, or Near Shore?

The decision on shorelines is an alternative, not a goal!

Contrary to popular press, the use of offshore resources or facilities is a choice that arises from the realignment goals and programs. When an organization seeks to move operations or services to a non-domestic location to take advantage of lower costs, superior delivery quality, or to address the need for continuous operations, the decision should be driven by the larger goal of profitability, customer service, or production provisioning. Those organizations, who establish a goal of moving products or services to foreign locations strictly due to savings in direct operating costs, will end up being disappointed by a host of direct and indirect consequences of their actions. This is very important so let me reiterate, utilizing over a decade of hands-on experience—the conclusion to use non-domestic workforces is a decision, and not an independent innovative relevance realignment goal.

Additionally, with global sourcing relationships more widespread, the business impact and risk being implicitly assumed by organizations has grown significantly. With continued global disruptions and chaos, all organizations need to examine both risk mitigation and business continuity plans for layers of masked risk within vendor and servicing relationships. The impact can create a ripple effect resulting in loss of jobs, profits, and untold litigation.

The utilization or adoption of any global model starts with unambiguous requirements linked directly to the business goals. These sets of requirements will dictate the operational model that needs to be employed to meet the stated program criteria and objectives (see *Figure 9.1*). The use of offshore relationships (whether internal or outsourced), must recognize the logistical, risk, cross-training, and cultural issues inherent within these choices and the others that will follow.

Onshore Augmentation
Most commonly delivered by offshore providers using individuals from their native country. Extensive use of visa's and working permits was widely utilized during the last decade to provide vertical skills sets at below market rates.

Service Aggregator
Domestic providers partner with offshore organizations to create a blended environment of personnel, services, and product specializations. Commonly used by service providers to expand their product lines while limiting their risks.

Partnerships and Acquisitions
Common since the turn of the millennium, numerous domestic firms have purchased offshore firms to lower their cost of services while improving their breadth and depth of delivery capabilities.

Channel Disintermediation
With the acceptance of a global workforce, businesses have by-passed traditional servicers and outsourcers for the establishment of their own multi-national workforce. Sometimes, these compete head-to-head with traditional channel providers.

Channel Catalyst
Large, diverse and efficient offshore firms have adopted an aggressive delivery model that provides quality and skilled personnel globally. Their models are adopted for "any shore" and they have expanded their offerings to serve a broad market base with unique and flexible products and services. They have created a >$15 billion market in just 15 years.

Figure 9.1—Offshore Models of Operation

Before your organization and teams make the decisions to utilize domestic or global workforces, a base appreciation of the market pressures, issues, and assessment models should be determined.

Market dynamics

The lure of international operations and use of low-cost resources have continually driven business functions for centuries. The markets created to offer these far-flung services and products has been motivated by the demands of trading blocs and treaties, political reforms, nationalistic expansions, regulatory changes, and competitive pressures (see *Figure 9.2*).

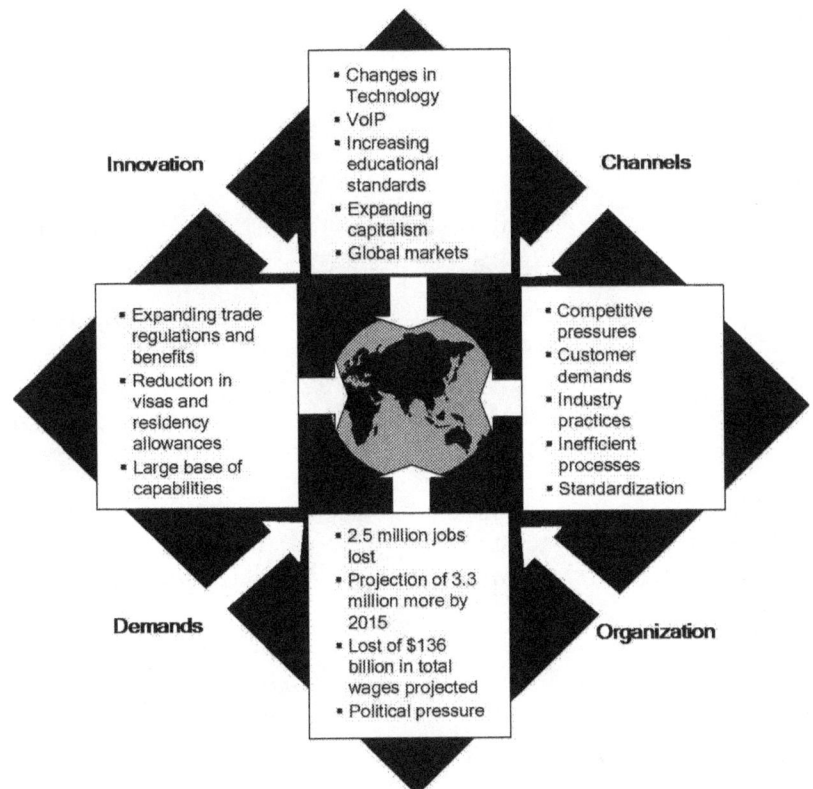

Figure 9.2—Drivers of International Economic Expansion

The primary catalyst for the rapid expansion and adoption of international markets and workers has been as a direct result of technology implementation. This assimilation of technologies, ancillary processes, and the education needed for operations, has been widely promoted by "developing countries" as an instrument for their local populations to improve their standards of living. Countries such as India, China, Russia, Romania, Peru, and Argentina have advanced programs in place to entice foreign corporations to utilize their domestic resources and companies. The success has been so pronounced that we are now witnessing these countries beginning to globalize their own work-forces to specialized firms, resulting in a "hierarchy" of offshore firms who utilize offshore firms.

The use of offshore firms will not go away. Yet, we are at a precipitous junction in how they are utilized, and the exact business benefits that can continue to be derived. For realignment program managers and their innovative relevance sponsors, they need to balance a plethora of particulars to arrive at an optimized solution set. These minimalistically include:

Standards: Global markets are growing increasingly focused on common productivity practices to hasten delivery and ensure consistency of results. Select offshore, onshore, and near shore organizations have unique offerings and proven records, while others are just beginning to gain the required experience.

Costs: The management of direct costs is usually what organizations base their decision on when selecting internal or external foreign workers and firms. On the other hand, the intangibles can greatly exceed the direct costs. Total cost of delivery must be assessed within and among the programs.

Concurrency: The maintenance of "dueling" workforces is seldom understood or analyzed. This condition is created by learning curve conveyance needs, which will be part of any startup or transition operation required for the adoption of a non-domestic workforce model. It can extend between 3 and 15 months depending upon the complexity of operations and transference of intellectual capital required.

Technology: Bewildering and accelerating changes permeate this area. The workforces' ability to adapt to these new offerings and how they materially affect the delivery, control, and management processes are substantial. Testing should not be underestimated.

Disintermediation: The channels for delivery, learning, and communication are fluid. The emergence of the global consumer has placed enormous pressure on the realignment programs to "get it right the first time." From experience, the ability to recover from the wrong choice or partner is less than 25% successful.

Atomization: The specificity of options, capabilities, and centers of excellences has created micro delivery channels filled with highly specialized providers. With a layering of foreign providers, this granular compartmentalization has produced delivery and legal liabilities for all corporations and innovative relevance realignment initiatives.

If you factor in domestic regionalization segmentations along with the foreign capabilities and requirements, you can now appreciate the complexity of the assessment processes for the utilization of offshore, onshore, or near shore resources. The decision is not the goal, but as we have seen it will materially affect the outcome and its obtainment.

Issues and misconceptions

Offshore. This single word conjures up great intrepidity with organizational personnel, and potential cost savings and risk management benefits from senior executives. Since the 1990's, it has been consistently estimated that up to 80% of the Fortune 500 used some form of offshore or outsourcing relationships, as budgets were tightened and qualified professionals became increasingly scarce. The cost of maintaining existing operations, coupled with over promising of returns by firms and consultants, has lead many a "c-level" executive to determine that these internally sustained competencies were not worth the headaches of daily oversight. As a result, organizations with their check book in hand signed their "non-core competencies" over to third-party providers. They in turn, delivered services or products at a set price for a period of 2 to 10 years. It seemed to be pretty straightforward? The principle belief was that the operational risks and burdens were minimized (via the outsourcing or offshore relationship), thereby allowing the organization to concentrate its focus on new markets, brands, and specializations.

Nevertheless, we have not learned from experiences of others, that these desires and promises seldom materialized as projected. Additionally, they did not meet the organizational expectations of improved flexibility and reduced oversight. Are your vendor relationships placing unwarranted risk on your organization? What are the caveats and misconceptions that we have witnessed from our decisions, which seek to satisfy a corporate goal?

Furthermore, not all offshore relationships are entered into willingly, nor are they visible to you the consumer, who purchases services from an outsourcer or a third-party provider. Take for instance a mortgage originator, who signs an operating deal to provide back office services (*e.g.*, IT processing, call centers, Internet commerce, and n-commerce) for their loans and those of their customers. Do they fully understand the servicing characteristics of the provider and where these tasks are being performed? Where has there been a shift in geographic servicing since the contract was signed? Have they examined the risks this relationship now places on the firm, shareholders, and the board? Are these services performed in a part of the world rife with turmoil, and heavily reliant upon a workforce that is 10,000 miles away separated by 15 hours in time zones? How much revenue is at stake, should the provider fail in their obligations due to worldwide events? What should they do?

We will examine the 10 most common issues and beliefs, which will have a pertinent influence on the realignment efforts, their programs of action, and how you can mitigate the perils of operation.

1. **"From a risk management perspective, we have contracts in place with clear escalation processes and procedures. International support creates no greater risks than having domestic resources."** In a perfect world this would be a truism. Still, not everyone believes that capitalism is positive (as the recent events in Russia can be a testament). What do you know about the records that are being sent across the boarders, and how are they retained or archived? What background checks are being performed on the personnel hired in these remote locations? Your organization needs to perform a due diligence on these at least yearly, as government and industry regulations on privacy, retention, data integrity, and liability can affect the legal exposure for the organization and its senior executives.

2. **"The impact to services from international delivery is a minimal risk as the global infrastructure provides redundancy of connectivity, and access to large skilled resource pools."** While the costs of international networks (price per trans Atlantic or Pacific line) has fallen over 35% in the last several years[xxvii], these communication lines can be up to 1/3 the total cost of delivering the services for the provider. Furthermore, the amount of time required obtaining and "provisioning" international lines can exceed 90 days even during periods of regional or global tranquility. What would happen if you were unable to get consistent service from the provider for more than 12 hours? 24 hours? As a consumer of these outsourced or offshore services, you must continually examine the fine print in their commitments to deliver connectivity. Alternate routing and fail over is complex, and it must be tested regularly. What proven "pathing," business continuity, and disaster recovery capabilities does your servicer provide? Is it tested and verified against your acceptance criteria?

3. **"From an economic standpoint, all functions and support knowledge should be placed offshore."** From a pure numbers perspective, this is a very attractive tenet to adopt. However, do you (or your customers) need to speak with skilled local personnel, who can answer questions and provide strategic leadership for definition, program management, and interface requirements? From experience, the total transference of skills to an offshore location creates an unworkable situation. Due to issues of process execution, time zones, cultural differences, subject matter experience, and basic human interaction, not all aspects can be ported to the least expensive location. A solid process (*e.g.*, CMM, ISO 9000, and Rational) must be in place **before** the migration can begin, and must be followed with accurate mid-course corrections as sustainable results are realized. Once in place, suitable metrics and measurements (performance, customer, program, and operational), will determine the personnel relationship mix (of domestic and offshore resources) that needs to be deployed.

4. **"Cultural support and integration of international personnel is not a factor, as we're only speaking of technical support and application development."** Let's examine the duties of our mortgage servicer. While technology skills can be taught quickly, do the personnel who are encoding the changes in a remote country understand the concept of a "variable annuity loan?" For example, in many countries, the concepts within the life cycle of a loan (including foreclosure) are unknown. These personnel must be educated and trained over a period of up to a year on the fundamentals and nuances of transferring this knowledge into sound procedures, rules, and operational principles. The system integration "touch points" represent interfaces that can completely disrupt the downstream information feeds needed by the organization's customer interfaces, data marts, and government reporting. This area of knowledge transfer and preparation is traditionally underestimated by offshore firms, and often overlooked by the purchaser of their services.

5. **"Global workers are more productive and willing to learn when compared to similar domestic workers."** We've all heard this from economists and even from noted global business leaders. It's just not the reality. A healthy mixture of a diverse workforce is needed to achieve optimal performance when considering global product and service delivery. Globalization of technology and servicing started in earnest in the mid 1990's with the realization of the Y2K challenges. It spawned an offshore industry that specialized with the remediation of old computer code in India, Moscow, and China, complete with foreign government sponsorship. This legacy has offered new opportunities to companies seeking to reduce the escalating cost of operations. In spite of this, due to culture differences and customs, the work habits and thought processes with international firms excel in some areas and fail in others. Much of the failure is due to a lack of appreciation by domestic companies on how to properly communicate, motivate, and integrate a global workforce.

6. **"Offshore partners only refer to those of the old Soviet Republics, China, and India."** With the post 9/11 days, we have seen a significant increase in organizations based overseas moving some of their staffs and functions to the North American continent. This is an excellent idea to help lessen the risk of natural or man-made disruptions, but it also can change the cost structures and interactions of the previously established business models. Now instead of dealing with a common location in an offshore city, your organization may be forced to subdivide their efforts across many time zones and nationalities to get the same level of servicing (albeit at a cheaper rate.) For you the customer, it should be transparent—it seldom is that simple. Investigate the interdependencies and relationships between the locations providing your services, as they are only as strong as the weakest link between them. The complexity of tracking and definition of metric measurements grows exponentially with the more geographic locations involved.

7. **External certifications (e.g., SAS 70 and Web Trust) ensure that service delivery is consistent across all providers regardless of where the service is conducted.**" Certifications need to be examined by you, the customer, for level of completeness and conditions of when the test was performed. For instance, on a SAS 70 there are various comprehensiveness levels that can be requested by the provider. When was the test performed and by who? Is the test still valid or has the operating environment and controls changed since evaluated? While these certifications are excellent, you cannot abdicate a complete and thorough due diligence in these areas. You must approach these as "buyer beware" and act accordingly. Also, each certification has a set function and limited scope of coverage. Can you articulate the differences? How do these contribute positively or negatively to your choice to select a provider for the services needed by your organization and paying customers?

8. **"It's the service provider's issue to deal with offshore partners and personnel as we're shielded from local customs and mores."** Incorrect. The primary burden is the providers, but what happens when there is an issue, production outage, escalation, communication failure, fraud, or breach of ethics? Remember, it is your information and the confidential records of customers at stake. Your customers entrusted their personal and financial privacy to you. In normal daily operations, you can be shielded a great deal from offshore personnel. When issues arise, you will have no choice to plan for the inevitable fact that you must have processes, procedures, and legal guidelines for these sometimes frequently occurring contingencies (production outages do happen). Make sure these contingent efforts and actions are determined before you sign the contracts. Don't wait for the traditional "100-day" offshore due diligence process (after the RFP and a letter of intent is signed) to address these risks. Otherwise, you may have a greater exposure and financial commitment than expected.

9. **"Operational activities cannot be moved offshore, if the processing center is based within the United States."** Five years ago, the technical ability to conduct remotely managed operations for servicing was difficult. Today, with advances from organizations like IBM, HP, SAS, Veritas, and other quality companies, combined with a growing worldwide plethora of fiber optic undersea cables, the vision has become a reality. With appropriate controls and technologies, offshore resources can reduce the cost of direct labor by up to 70%, when evaluated against comparable functions within the United States. It is an evolving option, now open to more organizations as the cost to value benefit can be effective for more than the Fortune 50. As a result, the ability to create a global "first shift" is possible, using follow-the-sun techniques that take advantage of time zone differences.

10. **"Structured processes are transplantable and transparent when instilling them in offshore personnel and organizations."** Unless you've actually attempted to implement and create an offshore entity using domestic processes, the statement appears to be completely logical. However, experience has demonstrated otherwise. Success with a global staff and service offering requires that processes be adopted to take advantage of the diverse workforce. You may transplant a consistent framework offshore, but failure to take advantage of the disparate in-country skills and learned behaviors, will result in performance disappointment, worker dissatisfaction, and lack of continual improvement. "Cookbook" approaches for offshore operations seldom work in global delivery. Although, the adoption of a strong framework (complete with definitive measurements) will lead to excellent productivity and end-customer satisfaction.

As you can determine, the ability to leverage an offshore business model is complex. As a purchaser of these services, you need to minimally examine your existing relationships to qualify and quantify the exposure. The industry trend is moving to a very competitive economic structure, where the cost per transaction is a primary differentiator. Only you, as a leader within the realignment effort, can determine the best innovative relevance alternative for your business and customers in support of the iterative programs created in Chapters 6 and 7. Globalization is here to stay, but not all providers have the rigor and discipline for operating consistently within the new business model.

Go-forward strategy

Innovative relevance recognizes and accepts the use of global resources to meet our customer, business, and shareholder requirements. The utilization of offshore or near shore resources can materially affect your margins, and hence your profitability. The choice to use global resources in the realignment effort must adhere to 10 tenets (see *Figure 9.3*).

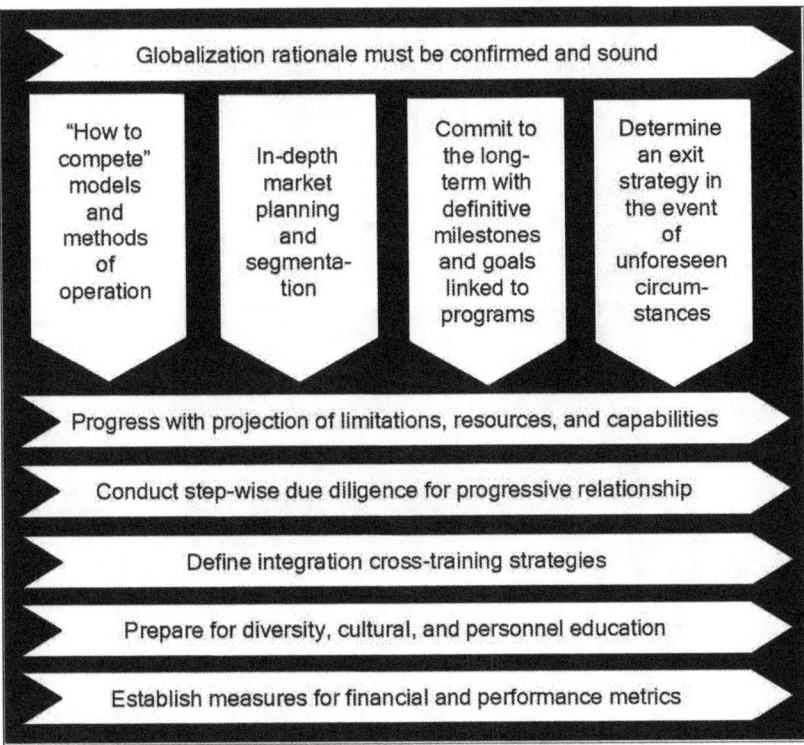

Figure 9.3—10 Tenets of Globalization

These tenets are useful guidelines and practices, which will provide you and the realignment team with careful consideration for the conclusions that will influence the organizational workforce (see Chapter 8). Regardless of the path taken, any conclusion must be profitable and realistic in order to sustain the continuous resources and support requirements necessary to make the programs successful.

A straightforward usage model for adopting onshore, offshore, or near shore resources in *Figure 9.4* may assist with the complex array of choices, which confronts the organization during their realignment efforts.

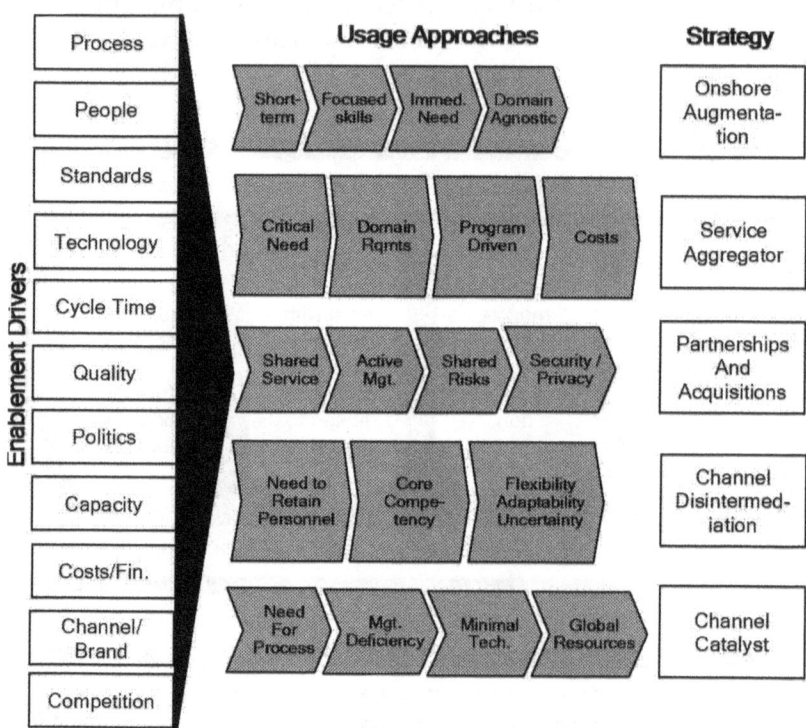

Figure 9.4—Go-Forward Strategies for Globalization

The strategy used for the execution of the realignment programs must be concentrated on the end results. The adoption of a global model requires the selection and implementation of structured, repeatable processes and supporting techniques. These will in turn bolster the standards needed for program completion, quality of delivery, and skill set transference.

The usage of integrated domestic and global models requires active and continuous supervision. Significant cross-training and domain transference will be a constant demand for the organization regardless of using augmentation staff, outsourcers, or your own personnel. The final determination of whether to use onshore, offshore, or near shore resources and production facilitates is not mutually exclusive. The amalgamation of these resources have the potential to provide substantial gains through reduced delivery costs, rationalized geographic channels, and increase margins.

The provisioning of an integrated globalized approach requires a combined channel strategy with specific roles and responsibilities tailored to customer preferences, brand economics, and organizational competencies. Furthermore, the organizational structure must be aligned with the new delivery requirements and coordination needs. The adoption of continuous improvement techniques and disciplines will be mandated to promote waste elimination, improved communications, and employee advancement.

Lessons learned

There is an inherent conflict of interest in asking internal personnel to realign their functions and groups to take advantage of global resources. Why would they willingly destroy or break-up the group that they have fought so hard to create? To properly utilize the decision making practices in this chapter, you'll need to ensure that you adhere to the realignment's approach for:

- What key processes should be adopted and improved, and which ones should be removed and outsourced (onshore, offshore, or near shore)?

- What are the baselines for the components (remember that for every dollar of capital spent today, you should expect to spend between $4 and $7 over the next three years to support any capital investment)?

- Has the organization identified, using established principles, goals, and objectives, what the programs will provide to the business and by what date?

Experience provides the axiom that the use of global resources or processes is seldom an "all-or-nothing" approach—contrary to popular press and management philosophies of the week. Globalization is determined by the organizational culture and critical competencies for sustainability. Follow-the-sun workforces can succeed, but they are delineated and assessed by more than just the direct costs or number of resources.

- Market dynamics can rapidly transform the economics and viability of any globalization effort. Contingencies must be accepted and implemented (see Chapter 14).

- The widespread usage of global resources to reduce on-going costs has been of significant benefit to customers and foreign economies. Nevertheless, the ability to compete must be measured in long-term sustainability, and risks of operation when deciding upon offshore location and resources.

- A tiered approached to globalization should be undertaken to ensure consistency of delivery, total cost of ownership minimization (it's not just for hardware), and achievement of the "To-Be" operational state (the cost to change an established offshore, outsourced facility can be significant).

- Careful consideration of the issues and risks will be required before investments, or long-term innovative relevance choices should be made to use onshore, offshore, or near shore resources or operations.

- Experienced models, personnel, and results from competitive or cross-domain globalization efforts should be benchmarked against proposed future state usage of internationally based operations.

Chapter 10

Focusing on Returns— Understanding Risks
Measurements cannot be disregarded

When our realignment programs loose track of the financial implications and returns promised by the innovative relevance initiatives, how can the sponsors continue to support and sustain the investments? How are the programs going to solve the primary goals and objectives set forth? Can these efforts be sustained without adequate financial controls and measures? Who is going to manage them? What should the organization expect the realignment programs to deliver? Will they live up to the expectations of the corporation, the people, the customers, the directors, and the shareholders?

The challenges with financial measurements created explicitly for realignment initiatives stems from the varied "primitive" metrics, which are contained with the programs and their correspondingly dependent projects. These primitives provide the discrete measurement levels needed to track, report, and guide the compartmentalized efforts. However, metrics need to be aggregated to provide the actionable operational information required to promote or correct program actions. The complexity of measurements resides not with their intent, but their precise definition, timing, and usage. Without a formalized and all-encompassing framework of metrics and measures by which to identify problem areas, benchmark program spans, and evaluate progress, the value on your investment can not be determined. Lacking appropriate metrics, the return to your realignment efforts will more likely reflect wishful thinking than reality.

Finding measurable and sustainable financial returns within some realignment programs and projects can be perplexing, even to disciplined and trained professionals. Nonetheless, only with the procedural establishment of full financial transparency can the realignment initiatives undertake significant capital and operating investments.

There is bona fide and concrete knowledge to be gained from rigorous investment analysis and tracking, but it will only become palpable if the organization is committed to the long-term, fervently focused, and politically agnostic. The definition and aggregation of financial measures starts with some basic questions.

1. Can the accuracy of the data be statistically measured?

2. What is the budget to actual variance of the effort?

3. Is the information generally accessible?

4. To what measure are the burden rates logically established?

5. Have performance standards been established?

6. If standard costs are employed, is there an established procedure for periodically revising them?

7. Are rework costs finitely measured and tracked?

8. Is there an internal or external audit of fiscal activities?

9. Are metrics analyzed by product or program differentiation?

10. Are measures classified by market or brand results?

11. Are gauges categorized by customer programs, results, and acceptance?

12. Are metrics arranged by territory or geographic region?

You should ask yourself these and other questions on the metrics being gathered within the innovative relevance programs and projects. Realignment measurements can be ineffective due to:

- potentially inadequate skills,
- lack of financial rigor,
- disorganized processes,
- internal political strife, and
- unrealistic deadlines.

Moreover, what specific business purposes are served by the realignment programs, and why are their measures continuing to be amassed? Have the programs transformed and now require innovative or altered measurement processes? What, precisely, are the metrics expected to present or promote? Better yet, how exactly, do they intend to influence or determine whether the realignment efforts are meeting the business expectations of the corporation (see Chapter 12)?

Once you have addressed these questions, your attention should now be turned to the internal mechanisms and measurements needed to facilitate the realignment initiatives.

Determining the investment analytics

In the late 1990's, the investments in realignment efforts were driven by technological and process improvements (often termed "corporate restructurings"). Although these investments promoted consistent delivery, integration, and greater production capabilities, the changing global business climates and unique customer demands were not incorporated into relevant metrics. Looking ahead, investments are not just motivated by a single customer or an application (*e.g.,* ERP, CRM)—they are driven by a need for improved profits, lower cost of ownership, shareholder actions, and a continuation of business operations in an unsympathetic commerce climate. Stringent measurements, complex processes, and most importantly a substantial return, drive today's investments when projecting the realignment's results and sustainability. The best innovative realignment solutions start with a robust information infrastructure (explained in depth in Chapter 11) for the sourcing of metrics.

Still, justifying the costs and projecting the returns associated with these program investments, requires a distinctive appreciation for the level of operating risk protection, and the bottom line yields these assets will deliver. As corporate leaders, we must continually examine the fundamental problems and inherent solutions haunting the creation of realignment valuations and profits. Comprehending the true need of the programs requires that we acknowledge the impact of potential failures on the organization's market, credit, and more important operational risks.

Furthermore, the availability and accuracy of knowledge regarding the total cost of ownership has been greatly overestimated. In general, personnel do a good job on lease/buy considerations and calculating the cost of capital. The short-fall has been with the projection of on-going personnel and operating costs for the investment. From practice, we have learned that the cost of capital is typically only one-fourth of the three year expected costs of ownership.

Defining an accurate ROI analysis for a business solution is not like calculating the returns used just a decade ago. Today, implementation requires various organizational changes, a discernment of new and existing process requirements, and the availability of financial data. These in turn, must incorporate the potential for the loss of top-line revenues and bottom line profits due to extra-ordinary operating risk. In general, the touchpoints and operating complexities are far greater than at any other time in history.

Personnel should begin by examining the market forces, technology trends, and operational risk guidelines, which affect their realignment program requirements. They must recognize the significance of market rejection for their programs, failure due to inadequate results, or misaligned investments in solution sets, which fail to provide improvements in quality, revenue, and customer acceptance. Investment analytics must be able to accurately capture, track, and assess the operational risks of delivering realignment programs throughout the enterprise. Since information and risk management is the core of any solid business realignment strategy, we must explore and create ways to unleash this information for team consumption.

Foundationally it is about acceptable risks

The risks inherent within realignment programs are segregated into four separate and distinct components, which must constantly be ascertained and assessed—credit, market, operational, and systemic.

Credit: Quantification of any risk dealing, which impinges on the enterprise's capabilities to administer finances, raise capital, and ensure cash-flow.

Market: Program measurements that directly and indirectly influence the organization's share price, financial perceptions, capitalization, regulatory needs, and shareholder's interests.

Operational: An area most affected by the realignment efforts. This includes relationships, personnel, technological, physical, financial controls, legal, production, and customer functional classifications.

Systemic: Measurements that deal with changes to processes and supporting systems. This may include alterations in applications, technologies, process inputs, outputs, infrastructures, and delivery sequences.

Moreover, risk analysis must address the hard to quantify components of customer confidence, potential sales loss, goodwill, undesirable market visibility, and relationship management. With the typical customer and shareholder perceptions that the organization's operations and production delivery is invulnerable to realignment disruptions, the long-term impact to sales, brand, and profitability (*e.g.*, market, credit, and operational risks) cannot be underestimated. Consequently, the capturing of primitive and summarized measures should be carefully considered, planned, and sourced to promote continuous reviews while enabling required adjustments.

One last risk that has to be mentioned is the cost of business disruptions, which need to be mitigated during the realignment programs. It should be noted that the traditional tracking, measurement, and calculation of business disruptions is not an IT (information technology) effort. It is a business-determined effort supported by IT. As an example, an IT support organization recently concluded that a 2-hour outage would cost the business $575,000, while the cost to fail over to a synchronous environment (*i.e.*, continuous availability) was over $1.2 million USD. Their deductions concluded that the technology investments required to diminish the outage probabilities (*i.e.*, risks) were not justified. When the analysis of the supporting assumptions and risk models were presented to the business sponsor, it was quickly substantiated that only generic industry metrics and models were utilized to reach IT's decision. When the correct organizational risk models driven by the business unit were applied, the cost of an outage exceeded $6 million per hour. Returns are more than just numbers. They must integrate the intangibles and acceptable operating risks that business personnel deal with everyday. For IT and the support they provide to the realignment initiatives to be effective, business-driven risk identification and responses must be included within their financial, quality, and organizational projections.

Experience creates success

It's important to be critical of vendor returns and risk projections. Many times, the vendor will provide "real world metrics" on the savings that can be achieved in a given industry segment when using their solutions. However, there are many undocumented assumptions that were used to create this public baseline or set of measures, which may not exist within your organization. In today's tight markets, vendors are very concerned with their competitor's products. As such, many times the metrics being offered have little to do with your situation as it does with their competitor's solution.

For accurate return computations, the use of outside professionals may be beneficial. Experienced professional services organizations can establish a comprehensive return model that accounts for varied risks, profits, and losses. Nevertheless, buyers need to understand that these organizations can fluctuate greatly in expertise. Not all professional services organizations have the skills necessary for developing, and implementing a plan designed for the changing alignment of information assets and high-level corporate objectives. Consequently, companies should engage those organizations who have spent years discerning these complex relationships, and who can utilize pragmatic "best practices" when establishing risk based return models.

Leading professional services organizations now offer a full spectrum of services—from simple backup and recovery to continuous availability solutions capable of yielding robust returns. Those who clearly understand how to efficiently manage operating expense over the life of the asset, economically integrate this into their contract terms. A premiere organization can assist with a comprehensive realignment plan that includes:

- Detailed risk assessments,

- Processes and procedures for continuity of operations,

- Business impact analytics and failure costs,

- Market and brand impacts and implications,

- Application and data availability plans,

- Customer acceptance and delivery consequences,

- Architecture, processes, and continuity testing preparations,

- Detailed design and implementation specifications,

- Comprehensive cost and return models, and

- Metric and measurement dashboards or portals integrated with corporate quality disciplines (e.g., Six Sigma, Balanced Scorecards).

Companies that implement a broad set of properly sourced measures can, with significant confidence, be assured that their realignment initiatives are constantly viable. Comprehensive measures can also reduce financial losses, while mitigating risk during the transitional activities. Additional benefits can include the minimization of interruptions for critical business operations, and the simplification of the decision-making process needed to fulfill stringent and changing legal, regulatory, and fiduciary obligations. Remember, if you can't measure it, you can't monitor it. If you can't monitor it, you can't influence it. If you can't influence it, you can't achieve realignment victory.

Lessons learned

The key to obtaining accurate realignment projections resides with knowing where the measurement starts. The establishment of a baseline is an essential building block that cannot be overlooked. This metric baseline provides the underpinning for measurement that must be made to ensure realignment projections are being realized. Only a complete realignment measurement solution can account for people, risks, probability of success, maintenance of multiple channels, and the total cost of ownership—which all impact returns. Companies that choose to base their realignment program investment decisions strictly on the cost to purchase/lease, installation, insurance, setup, salvage, monthly maintenance, or fair market value, will end up making a very expensive mistake for at least the next three years.

- The measurement of realignment programs is not founded upon a single metric or measurement program.

- Program measures must account for the varied nature and integration needs of primitive metrics to guarantee a correct assessment of progress.

- Measures and metrics must be balanced with organizational maturity, culture, and realignment needs before selecting "best practices" or benchmarks to ascertain progress.

- Investment analytics need to determine total cost of ownership (beyond the hardware and software) when projecting program saves, revenue improvements, or profits.

- Risk management will be a critical analytic adjustment factor when evaluating progress and results. Risks may offset the measures with yet unrealized problems or benefits that will alter the programs' delivery.

- Investment analytics must be challenged. Their historical usage within the enterprise may not meet the same assumptions or usage characteristics that were in effect during the operation of the "As-Is" state. The "To-Be" projections and transition states may materially affect their validity and enforceability.

- Experienced personnel or outside consultants will be needed to promote a comprehensive linkage of primitive metrics, summarized metrics, and supporting measures for program heuristics, forecasting, and tracking.

Chapter 11

Utilizing End-to-End Informational Management

A proactive approach for continuous analysis

The execution and tracking of innovative relevance programs is concentrated around accountability. This accountability requires not only superior personnel, but defined processes integrated with the required information for accurate decisions. Yet, the accuracy of information is transitory. The importance of information used within a realignment program only has value for a set period of time. After this time, conclusions made utilizing this information can lead to erroneous actions and investments.

The End-to-End Informational Management (E2EIM) process within realignment programs can yield significant returns due to the definitive sourcing of information, and recognition that information has a "shelf-life." The use of E2EIM represents the active management of information. This information is used to create dashboards, portals, metrics programs, and for reporting, to name but a few. At its core, is an integrated model that links the informational sources together, while it tracks their usage and summarization for inclusion into ancillary support environments (see *Figure 11.1*).

E2EIM provides a storehouse of information that can be utilized to capture artifacts. These data sources can include; interview results, captured images, recordings of electronic collaborative meetings, program plan updates, resource schedules, and financial results, while supplying input to business intelligence systems, electronic dashboards, measurement systems, and web portals. A key and often overlooked requirement is that over 85% of the information generated by realignment programs resides within "unstructured" data. Historically when we think of data or information, we focus on application systems, program offices, spreadsheets, financial systems, or desktop support systems—data within the ever growing localized repositories stuck on those hard disk drives. The problem with these traditional data sources is that less than 15% of corporate information resides in these "structured" formats.

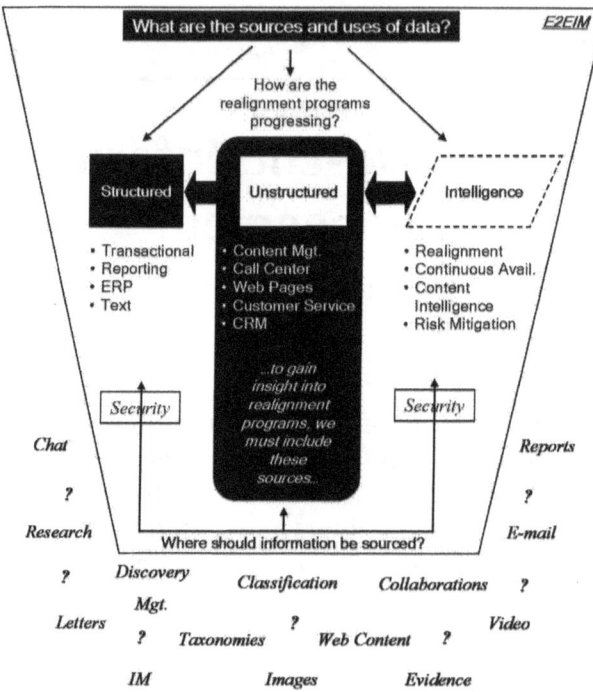

Figure 11.1—Innovative Relevance Informational Sources

The sources and uses of information within realignment programs can no longer be focused on a program office, application systems, or with a single individual or team. Additionally, E2EIM also recognizes the integration and disposal of information as the program's progress.

The inclusion of many new, non-traditional, and unstructured sources has been the focus of continual regulatory scrutiny since 2000. Unstructured data applicability to restructuring efforts must not be ignored, and should adhere to similar treatments for structured data due to the potential impact on production, customers, markets, and financial results.

A model of integration

The integration of informational assets within the realignment effort requires a "meta" model, or data about the data, for information sources and uses. Plainly stated, we need to create a series of informational relationships between the realignment definition, the baseline, the assessments, the migration plans, and the programs being undertaken (see *Figure 11.2*). These relationships can be easily created by an internal or external information technology staff or outsourcer. The primary drivers for the interrelationships are determined using the framework presented in this book along with your discrete organizational needs, industry drivers, regulatory requirements, and process demands.

For this repository to be effective, it should be created using a logical design. The design is produced after the realignment effort has been funded, but before the baseline process has begun. This model will recognize the informational needs that must be captured and transmitted from the realignment efforts to promote improvements, financial conformance, and resource allocations. The representation is also an excellent method for incorporating unstructured informational elements and artifacts. The inclusion of these non-traditional sources provides the program team's valuable insight into ancillary activities and interdependencies, which need to be managed to control risks and for sustainability of their efforts. In addition to the direct information related to the team's individual efforts, the collection of these sources allows for use of advanced analysis and assessment techniques and tools.

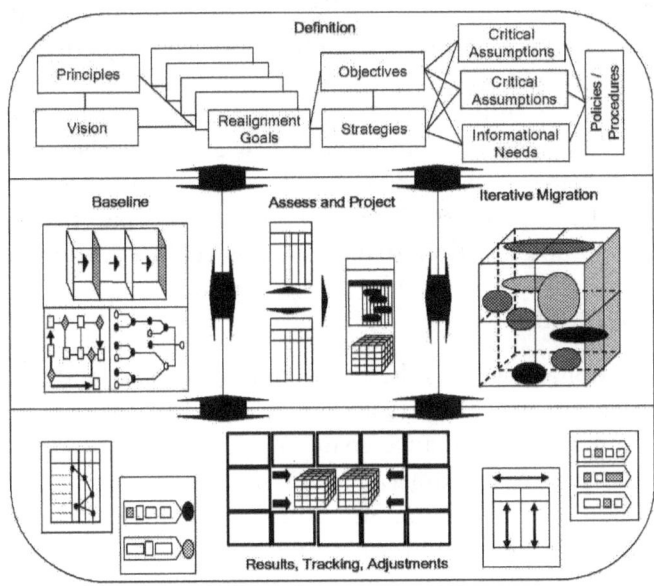

Figure 11.2—Realignment Repository

With the logical storehouse of information complete, the establishment of a physical technological environment should be undertaken. Use of standard database and data warehousing products and methods will be invaluable. Once the physical repository environment is created, registration needed for appropriate baseline associations, fit-gap analysis, and program projection can be conducted. This registration provides the team with a powerful "what-if" analysis along with structured associative capabilities. Use of tools involving data mining, business intelligence, and pattern recognition can be employed with unparalleled accuracy and predictability.

The creation of a realignment repository provides its own, internal audit trail. This journaling and auditing capability is an inherent benefit that promotes due diligence, repeatability, and dynamic correction in the event of flawed artifact sourcing. Furthermore, it can provide the team with the capabilities to produce multiple scenarios, which will lead to superior decision making abilities, higher confidence intervals, and a potential to realize the goals sooner.

The design of the repository must be flexible and adaptable, to ensure it can be kept relevant with new innovations or modifications to the baseline assumptions for all realignment initiatives. It is strongly suggested that use of iterative or extreme delivery techniques be used to launch the endeavor. Once underway and proven, a more formalized migration with improved procedural guidelines should be added to "bullet-proof" the repository before general usage by the enterprise.

The physical design of the repository must account for new data types that will be unplanned when first conceived. As new team members are added and programs adopted, they will promote new data sources that assist with realignment success and completeness. These data types will span three taxonomies or classifications of information; structured, unstructured, and intelligence.

Structured information

This informational source is the most commonly used and understood by teams and organizations. The extraction of data from applications such as ERP, CRM, manufacturing, finance, materials management, provisioning, and human resources are commonplace. While these applications are useful, they have limited value in determining future needs, providing assessment projections, and understanding significant components of the baselining environment. They are, generally speaking, operational processes that have been programmed and computerized. Structured information can be defined as:

Information sourced from traditional automated processes such as applications, reports, forms, spreadsheets, and data files. This information follows predetermined formats, arrival rates, volumes, and channels.

The use of structured information is very valuable when utilizing statistical analysis to determine variation within products and services. Structured information can assist with problem determination when employing root-cause analysis techniques. Historically, program offices employed to track large initiatives were solely concentrated on gathering structured data about initiative progress (*e.g.*, estimates to completion, time reporting, budgets, and actuals)—the needs of the organization have changed their data collection requirements.

The challenge of utilizing structured information for realignment programs includes:

1. Increasing volumes across disparate technological platforms,

2. Highly complex business issues are not represented within the current associations,

3. Conflicting data leads to refutability of sources—"which version of the truth?" is valid?

4. Functional and technical experts have little time for changes, adjustments, extractions, manipulations, and questions,

5. Staff downsizing and attrition has lead to a skills void, and

6. Older systems and processes cannot be extrapolated to meet the classifications and segmentation required by "To-Be" models and projections.

In spite of this, while this information needs to be captured and analyzed by the realignment efforts, there is a greater foundation of data that must be sourced and synthesized if we are to be successful. The use of unstructured information is at the central point of baseline, assessment, and iterative migrations being adopted within the realignment programs.

Unstructured information

Unstructured information has existed for over 40 years. However, it's only recently that we have been able to efficiently integrate and synthesize these sources of information for artifact analysis and decision making. The widespread use of the Internet has delivered ubiquitous and unstructured mediums, communications, and dispersal systems. These constantly changing systems and message vehicles represent fundamental and irrevocable methods of new informational sources, which will be used by our personnel, customers, alliances, and shareholders.

It has been estimated that up to 85% of all corporate information lies within unstructured sources that include:

• E-mail/notes	• Contact Centers
• Video	• Blogs
• Content Management	• Images
• Web Pages	• Chat/instant messaging
• Customer Service	• Collaboration
• Presentations	• Letters/documents

New "data types" are constantly being introduced. Furthermore, the sources listed above will need to be further decomposed into granular components to be useful in realignment analysis. Unstructured information has a wealth of content that typically constitutes the majority of the value for the project teams.

For these reasons, the repository is more about the integration and management of unstructured informational sources than traditional data management warehouses. The realignment teams' success will be directly tied to their ability to use this information, and unlock it from the data sourcing artifacts. These artifacts may include one of those mentioned above, or maybe enclosed in new "containers."

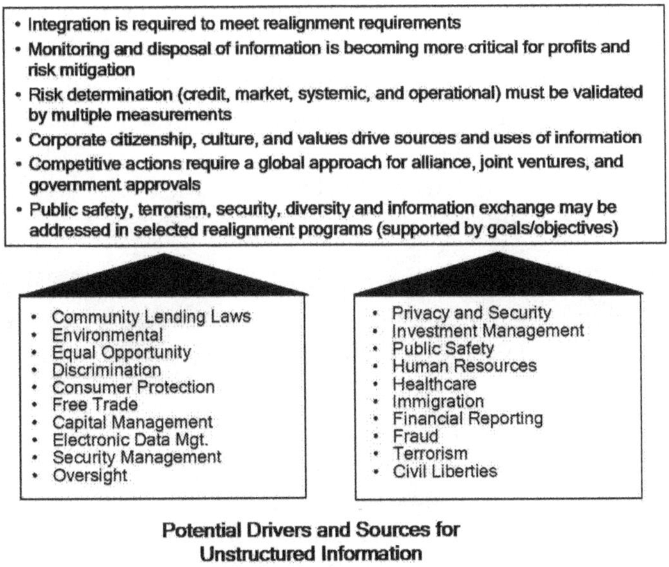

- Integration is required to meet realignment requirements
- Monitoring and disposal of information is becoming more critical for profits and risk mitigation
- Risk determination (credit, market, systemic, and operational) must be validated by multiple measurements
- Corporate citizenship, culture, and values drive sources and uses of information
- Competitive actions require a global approach for alliance, joint ventures, and government approvals
- Public safety, terrorism, security, diversity and information exchange may be addressed in selected realignment programs (supported by goals/objectives)

- Community Lending Laws
- Environmental
- Equal Opportunity
- Discrimination
- Consumer Protection
- Free Trade
- Capital Management
- Electronic Data Mgt.
- Security Management
- Oversight

- Privacy and Security
- Investment Management
- Public Safety
- Human Resources
- Healthcare
- Immigration
- Financial Reporting
- Fraud
- Terrorism
- Civil Liberties

Potential Drivers and Sources for Unstructured Information

Figure 11.3—Potential Drivers and Sources of Unstructured Information

Other unstructured informational sources and influencers can be obtained from outside the corporation. These informational drivers can have a material affect on the baseline analysis and assessment projections (see *Figure 11.3*). Information derived from external sources will need validation, and potential cleansing to guarantee conformity and applicability. In technical circles, the inclusion of unstructured or structured data into a collective repository requires a process known as "extraction, transformation, and loading" or ETL.

The use of unstructured information will involve the use of data "cubes," or three dimensional models to properly link the encapsulated informational "nuggets" embedded within their boundaries. Being able to tap this unstructured information demands skilled personnel who are trained in its treatment and blending. These skill sets are invaluable within the realignment support team, as their unique and focused intelligence analysis methods and techniques materially contribute to the innovative relevance programs' diagnostic integration capabilities.

Intelligence analysis

With an unambiguous comprehension and combination of structured and unstructured informational sources, the innovative relevance teams can begin to forecast and make informed decisions utilizing its contents. You can now see the real purpose of the repository is more about our ability to integrate, predict, and track our realignment efforts rather than just sophisticated use of technology. Our E2EIM sources and uses provide an enablement or catalyst effect promoting program reassurance and relevancy, rather than using innovation for the sake of innovation.

One relevant use of innovative technology is in the area of repository intelligence. The use of data mining coupled with multidimensional analysis provides:

> An ability for the innovative relevance teams to consolidate, view, and analyze information in multiple dimensions to elevate comprehension of varied data sources within elements of time.

The capability to aggregate the artifacts and sources of information allows for complex relationship associations to be created. This analysis can be conducted using off-the-shelf business or context intelligence tools.

With the combination of informational sources, intelligent induction analysis techniques, visualization, statistical analysis, and even neural networks can be employed depending upon the quality and integrity of the information gathered. As it can be deduced, intelligence analytics is not a one-time event. It utilizes iterative and exploratory techniques to validate or dispel realignment programs and directions using objective, multifaceted informational sources. This analysis promotes accurate clarity for investments, measurements, and tracking needed to deliver profits (see *Figure 11.4*).

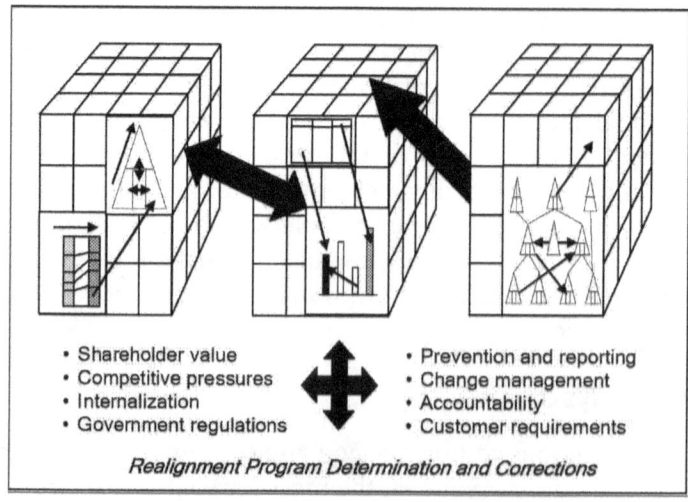

Figure 11.4—Intelligent Analytic Techniques

The exact level and sophistication of intelligence analysis is as individual as innovative relevance realignments are unique. The use of an informational repository must be aligned with the culture, disciplines, and skill set abilities of the projected "To-Be" organization. Critical questions need to be answered by the realignment leader and their sponsors:

- What degree of information integration is being sought?
- What are the risks and/or rewards for achieving realignment?
- Can the organizational culture support the needs of the realignment and its informational requirements?
- Where do we begin and how do we sustain it?
- What level of complexity warrants the use of intelligence analytics?
- Can we leverage our existing investments in personnel, software, and techniques?
- What is the cost of implementing the informational repository?

It should also be noted that the construction of the storehouse provides a workable foundation for iterative migrations as discussed in Chapter 7. The linking of informational sources allows for an "Evergreening" of programs, while accounting for variations in business, industry, and technology. The use of intelligent analytical techniques leverages the informational repository to promote "out-of-the-box" thinking with quantifiable organizational resource requirements. Without an End-to-End Informational Management (E2EIM) repository, the process of defining, projecting, and tracking life-cycle source usage can become monumental.

Lessons learned

Information is only an opinion until it is sourced, measured, and applied. The use of an integrated E2EIM for realignment efforts is essential with the substantial volumes of information available within a corporate environment. The rationale and success factors needed to be able to employ intelligence informational sourcing analysis includes:

1. Information repository management (*i.e.*, E2EIM) is a process—it can start today.

2. E2EIM promotes integration of workflows and business processes.

3. It is not just about products or technologies.

4. It requires integration, preplanning, and alignment.

5. It mandates specialized skill sets with proven, hands-on experience.

6. A comprehensive method to integrate structured and unstructured informational sources.

7. It will materially influence realignment programs.

8. E2EIM decreases silo specificity and skill fragmentation, while allowing for broader analytical reviews.

9. It is not free.

10. It is not instantaneous.

SECTION 4

IMPEDIMENTS—MANAGING THE CHAOS

"Till the war-drum throbbed no longer, and the battle-flags were furled..."
—Alfred Tennyson

Change can sometimes be thought of as organized chaos. Within innovative relevance initiatives, unchecked chaos can result in program failure. Impediments within the programs can manifest themselves subtly or aggressively hostile. With very few exceptions, impediments have to be measured against the risk posed to the realignment initiatives, rather than the methods by which they are uncovered. In this section, we examine methods to identify and lessen the chaos before it starts. We'll also whimsically look at seven typical chaos models, while addressing the need to maintain day-to-day consistency throughout the realignment initiatives.

Chapter 12: Management of Expectations

Chapter 13: Regulatory Challenges

Chapter 14: Day-to-Day Must Remain Viable

Chapter 15: The Seven Deadly Sins

Chapter 16: "...A Flea in One's Ear..."

Chapter 12

Management of Expectations
In the absence of information, someone will create it

In corporate life, we talk about "exceeding expectations", "meeting expectations", or even "missing expectations." We use these phrases in evaluating personnel, analyzing programs, measuring financial results, understanding market perceptions, or even defining customer interactions. Made famous by consultants, market gurus, and management soothsayers, expectation management is grounded within the human psyche and our organizational cultures.

For realignment efforts, the need to establish results is more than just immediate numerical efficiency and bottom line profits. The organization needs to embrace the positive aspects of the transformations in order to assimilate them into their daily operational models and processes. The vehicle needed to move us from the "As-Is" environment to a "To-Be" projection is inherently fixed within the realignment's continuous communication and organizational level-setting requirements.

Expectation management is not a "one-off." It is not about setting the goals and objectives, and then "performing unnoticed for the next 11 months." Expectation management is a critical strategy to mitigate the chaos created by modifications to workers activities and daily processes. As we discussed in Chapter 7, the need to compartmentalize the programs into self-contained and distinctive priorities with durations that do not exceed 120 days, will be a catalyst for success. By combining these shortened, yet logically self sufficient efforts with strong communication initiatives, the success of the innovative relevance programs have been greatly enhanced.

Furthermore, the achievement of suitable expectations requires the team to determine the appropriate blend of program relevance, innovation, and realization with the organization's ability to understand and act upon the changes. This balance requires careful consideration of the baseline, to determine the vehicle for communications necessary to reach the targeted and segmented corporate audiences (see *Figure 12.1*).

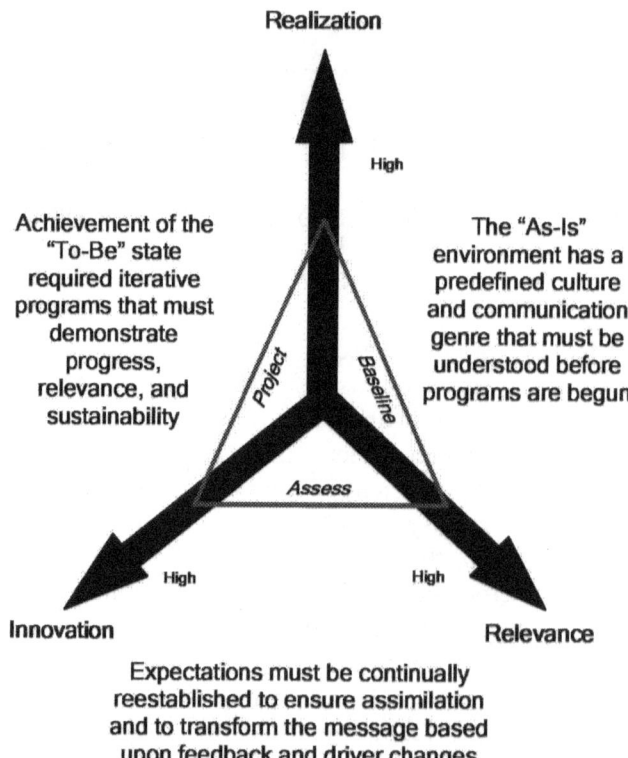

Figure 12.1—Constraints must be Balanced and Reinforced

The intersection of these triple constraints determines the "coverage map" essential to promote acceptance, organizational internalization, and on-going dialogue. The use of the triple constraints must continually be analyzed, before activities to set expectations are undertaken. This is due to the shifting nature of the expectations, the frequency or nature of those communications, and the risk-adversity intrinsically contained by the organizational culture.

The relative nature of expectations

Expectations have an offensive habit of continually changing during a realignment effort. These differences can be attributed to:

Initial reactions: During the early stages before the realignment has begun, expectations usually reside at one of two extremes. They can be very pessimistic believing that changes will bring about unnecessary new processes, procedures, loss of freedoms, job cuts, and so on. Conversely, they can be overly optimistic with unattainable goals and unrealistic timeframes for transformation. These initial expectations tend to last between 30 and 60 days until the baselining efforts are in progress and producing deliverables. Communication methods usually employed include town hall sessions, enterprise press releases, focusing groups, and strategic interviews. These "wait-and-see" expectations are displaced once the results begin to be produced and assessed by the organizational culture (*i.e.*, the grapevine).

Success: Depending upon the political alliances within the managerial culture, success can bring significant converts towards the realignment program, while strengthening the resolve and determination of those willingly embracing the innovative relevance initiatives. The management of expectations must be controlled to properly maintain projected results without unbridled enthusiasms. The downside of success is that the detractors of the realignment will go "underground" to become conscientious objectors using passive-aggressive actions. Success must be tempered with supplementary communications to control unwarranted outlooks—necessary to guarantee the establishment of an accurate, on-going results environment.

Failure: While we all despise the thought of being unsuccessful, it does happen with ill-defined programs, or those that failed to utilize a prioritized model for execution (see Chapter 7). When events deliver less than anticipated and promised, don't hide them. Put the "spin in the washer," and not on the realignment efforts. Nothing will set a constant barrage of negative expectations more than covering up difficulties experienced by realignment efforts. Those political detractors that are either actively aggressive or passively aggressive towards the achievement of the "To-Be" projection will reap lasting benefits when failures are "positively" spun. This area is where the ethics and integrity of your team will come into question, and they should be exemplary. Negative expectation management begins with getting out in front of the situation, before others can be allowed to further their personal agendas. Remember; be humble, but lead courageously in these circumstances.

Additional expectation variations can be attributed to programs that are late. In these cases, it is not a failure (not yet), but these programs are experiencing difficulties with resources, increased risks, and unmet dependencies, to name just a few. These constraints should be constantly monitored and presented to the sponsors as part of the normal course of program management. If they continue and are unresolved, then it will be mandatory that the project team, realignment leader, and/or sponsors all get in front of the organization to deal with potential ramifications and naysayer's. Depending upon the criticality and impact, board members or their respective committees may also need to be consulted to level set their expectations.

As we discussed in Chapter 8, the training and education of personnel can have a profound affect on their expectations for the realignment initiatives. A required curriculum for all retained employees should be a session on the innovative relevance programs, their timeframes, and their implications. It should be put in context of the organizational goals and principles established as the critical drivers for the realignment efforts.

Additionally, the age, corporate responsibility, and experience all have a great deal to do with individual and department level expectations. The communication messages used to set the expectations must be presented at a "plane of commonality" for the audience. A generic, across the board message delivered in a single format, may not achieve the discrete, sought after effects. Repeatability using alternative channels (just like we do for our products and services), will be required. To properly manage expectations, a "one-size fits all" approach is not recommended. While this involves more work effort and sometimes lengthens the program duration, it is a mandatory requirement, which if not met will yield chaos (see Chapter 15) and reduced productivity.

Vehicles of communication

The methods or "vehicles" by which to establish, reinforce, and moderate expectations can take many forms. We are most familiar with the often poorly planned meeting[xxviii]. All the same, like any vehicle that transports you or products on roads to reach a given destination, each one is designed for a specific purpose, audience, or workload (*see Figure 12.2*). Additionally, the use of individual or combined communication methods depends upon the point in time of the realignment initiatives. Early on, extensive use of multiple structured meetings will be required to reach out and associate with targeted corporate employees. As the successes are achieved and realignment goals are being realized, a more quantitative and printed form of communication may be just as effective.

The correct format and form of expectation management must also consider the feedback or reality attained from prior efforts. Blind adherence to a set format due to familiarity is reckless for the programs. The audience is seeking to place the messages, using their listening receptors, into contextual segments familiar or important to them. The reaction and feedback provided during the expectation delivery process, will greatly improve the chance of positively influencing the audience's knowledge and the receptiveness of the innovative relevance programs.

A critical dysfunctionality that can occur within realignment teams is what we term "realignment arrogance." It takes the form of superiority, entitlement, and blind ambition. It will transform the positive management of expectations into uncompromising vehicles of coercion, distrust, and pervasive organizational anxiety. Team members, who display this arrogance, must be quickly challenged and educated on the goals of realignment, along with the appropriate methods to sustain organizational transformation and profitable results.

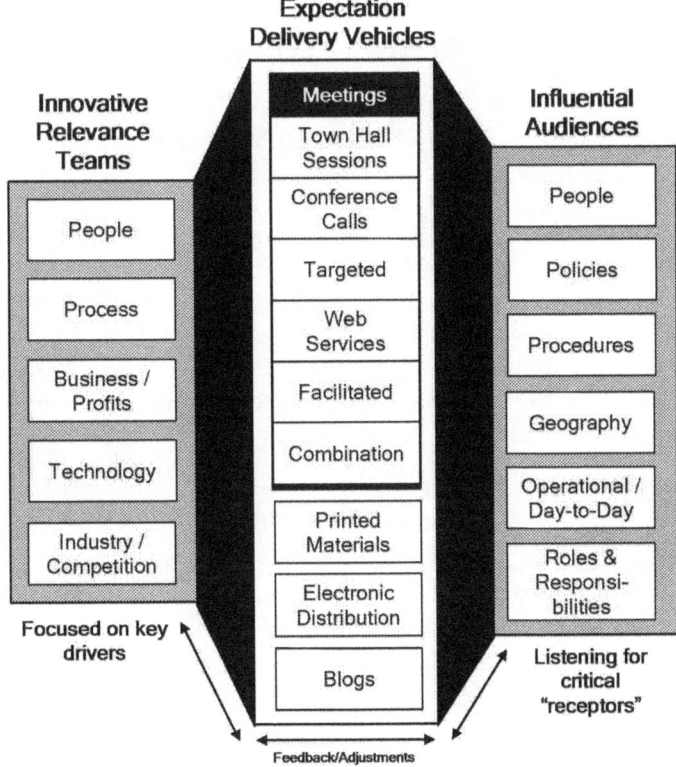

Figure 12.2—Realignment Communication Methods[xxix]

Let explore the attributes of the expectation management delivery vehicles demonstrated in *Figure 12.2.*

Town Hall: Used by executives to reach out to large corporate audiences. It provides a forum for them to communicate their intent for realignment initiatives, while taking questions from the floor. This format typically uses a combination of presentation materials, a lecture format, and Q&A. They are conducted geographically and personally.

Conference Calls: Common since the 1970's, when advanced phone systems allowed for the integration of multiple simultaneously active phone lines. These audio based formats are effective with limited audiences who have a pre-distributed agenda, materials, and expectations. They are good for follow-up, repetitive formats, and reinforcement. They are not well suited for initial meetings, corrective actions, or "bad-news." Now combined with VoIP services, these formats can include video and content delivery. If using VoIP services, the format can be expanded to include broader and diverse audiences.

Targeted: These meetings are the most familiar, and are used extensively to influence, guide, or communicate directions to a small group. Pre-established agendas and desired outcomes should be determined in advance.

Web Services: A host of new, web based communication methods have been devised, and are being widely adopted by many corporations. These services provide integrated voice, video, and document sharing across geographically dispersed groups. They are excellent methods to reach out to a global workforce when local proximity cannot be obtained.

Facilitated: Sometimes these are referred to as "moderated" sessions where a third-party assists with the delivery of critical messages. Third-party individuals are highly trained in group dynamics, are skilled in realignments, and have a sound ability to think on their feet in front of sometimes hostile audiences. They are used as a "go-between" to diminish political adversaries, and ensure the audiences are receptive to the realignment programs.

Combination: The utilization of several approaches at the same time to reach a broader and diverse audience composition. For example, a realignment leader may choose to hold a town hall session with the largest group of employees, while establishing a web services link to four other remote sites. Additionally, separate audio feeds may be sent to plant floors where high speed Internet access is unavailable. At the same time, she may have invited a "guest" facilitator who acts as the moderator to provide the "prompts" for her, her staff, and real-world examples of why the realignment effort can succeed.

Printed Materials: When employing traditional printed copies for distribution, the use of preprinted professional messages may be advantageous (*e.g.,* use of a CMYK offset service). This may include the hiring of a marketing firm or branding agent to provide the themes that can promote, market, and sell the idea of restructuring.

Electronic Distribution: While most of us use e-mail, the establishment of dynamic web pages, videos, distributable and annotated presentations, may also be employed.

Blogs: Also referred to as web logs or blogging, it is a recent Internet communication technique that is gaining wide acceptance. In its simplest form, web authors (*i.e.,* a realignment leader), can place information on an internal web site discussing and presenting the transformation programs. Visitors can then respond to the posting, and a dialogue will then pursue. Subsequent visitors can read the internal postings thereby allowing them to respond creating a "thread." This technique has shown great promise for establishing commonality, generating ideas, and highlighting trouble spots before they are seen on the bottom line.

As you can see, the selection of a delivery vehicle for the management of expectations has much to do with the messages, audiences, and capabilities possessed by the organization and the speaker. It is always more effective to start simple, test your messages, and then reach out to a larger audience using more elaborate and sophisticated combinations. Don't forget, repetition to manage the expectations of the organization and its culture is a "good thing."

Organizational culture

The existing culture of an organization cannot only have a material and direct impact on program performance; it can also influence the acceptance of key messages to personnel and suppliers. These organizational cultures can run the gambit from amenable to outright hostile. The cultural characteristics will be determined using interviews, artifacts, and other information sources, as part of the baselining process of realignment (see Chapter 5).

Nonetheless, a realignment practitioner should be aware of the organization's cultural classifications that they may encounter, and the impediments that can manifest as the teams achieve expectation alignment.

Authoritative: In more familiar terms, a command and control structure. All major decisions permeate from the top-down with little room for individual thinking, collaboration, or "out-of-the-box" approaches.

Customer Centric: An organization dedicated to customer satisfaction, delivery, and accessibility. These organizations employ collaborative solutions with customers in terms of supply chains, product quality, designs, and informational linkages. They have also assimilated customer measurement programs to drive out variability (e.g., Six Sigma, ISO, and CMM).

Decentralized: These cultures empower their individual managers with significant decision making capabilities and discretionary financial autonomy. Personnel in these organizations have a high degree of self satisfaction, and tend to promote high performance teams.

Fear and Terror: Some organizational cultures believe that conflict and terror can be excellent motivational tools. They strive to create chaos to promote a "survival of the fittest," believing that the strong will prevail and the organization will profit. Unconstructive politics and cut-throat behaviors are commonplace.

Performance Driven: These goal setting organizations promote internal cohesion using measurable objectives at a department level. These performance organizations are driven towards results. Their models of operation are highly collaborative and self correcting.

Blended Cultures: Within an organization there may exist several divergent and even opposing cultures. These are usually as a result of mergers or acquisitions. These cultures tend to survive until the next M&A[xxx] activity when a new culture is adopted into the "blended family." These fragmented cultures result in lengthened program delivery timeframes, extensive expectation management, and conflicting realignment guidelines.

The organizational community can also present two "faces." On one front, the culture publicly shown can be that of adherence, commonality, and strength of purpose. On the other hand, this outward facing culture needs to be examined and tempered with results, definitive communications, and private actions (*i.e.*, patterns of behavior). This secondary or true face of the organization tends to pose the greatest problems for realignment efforts. If it is "negatively" charged, it can passively shield an undercurrent of resistance that will stymie the innovative relevance initiatives. If "positively" charged, this culture can be a great asset for the sponsors of the realignment and their sustaining transformation teams.

Always keep in mind that organizational cultures do not change overnight. Regardless of the merits and benefits that can be derived by the realignment efforts, organizational cultures cannot and will not succumb to material behavioral adjustments easily. Only with measured programs, definitive action steps, and constant and repetitive expectation management can the organizational culture be influenced to sustain the proposed realignment modifications.

Lessons learned

The use of expectation management is not simple. It requires significant practice and proven experience when conducting realignment initiatives. The variables of deployment fluctuate widely as the realignment programs progress and results of prior communications are measured. Key lessons include:

- Frequent, multi-channeled strategies to reach out to the corporation, alliances, and partners must be developed.

- Adjustments to communication strategies must be made based upon feedback to promote receptive adherence to realignment goals and objectives.

- Expectation management requirements will change as the realignment efforts progress.

- Expectation management is not a one-time event.

- Communication constraints need to be documented, and then balanced to meet the needs of innovative relevance programs.

- Expectation management is grounded in the teams' ability to understand and empathize with the affected audiences.

Chapter 13

Regulatory Challenges—Impediments to Success?

Compliance mandates will not subside—prepare for the bureaucrats!

Round-trip trades, bogus financial reports, off sheet items, collusion, improper oversight, lack of regulatory reviews, inadequate controls, and countless criminal actions have resonated in the financial headlines for the last five years—and we're not finished. It appears that we've gone back over 80 years to a time when Wall Street can no longer be trusted, and where profits are artificially driven by the need for quarterly returns and results. Our faith in corporate leadership and the financial markets has been non-existent amid a languishing stock market and worldwide turmoil.

To improve confidence, our market regulators have increased compliance requirements at a blistering pace during the same five year period—exceeding a 15% annualized rate. Presently, there are over 15,000 state, federal, and local regulations within the United States. Add to this the European Union's requirements, foreign states, and tough religious requirements, the risks and limiting factors for innovative relevance programs continue to become multifaceted.

During the last 25 years, we have witnessed an evolution leading up to today's crisis of confidence with our corporations (see *Figure 13.1*). Consequently, innovative realignment efforts need to satisfy not only integrity and ethical guidelines (see Chapter 2), but we need to meet the highest levels of scrutiny imposed by regulatory agencies, self-regulating organizations (SRO's), and politicians when crafting and performing iterative realignment migrations.

147

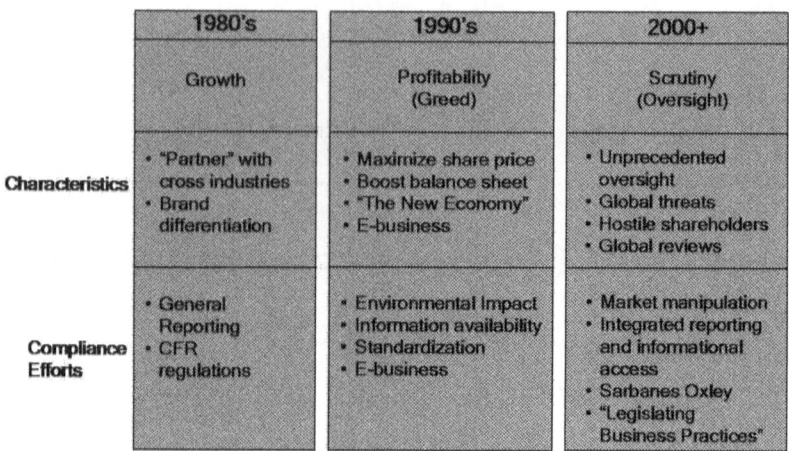

	1980's	1990's	2000+
	Growth	Profitability (Greed)	Scrutiny (Oversight)
Characteristics	• "Partner" with cross industries • Brand differentiation	• Maximize share price • Boost balance sheet • "The New Economy" • E-business	• Unprecedented oversight • Global threats • Hostile shareholders • Global reviews
Compliance Efforts	• General Reporting • CFR regulations	• Environmental Impact • Information availability • Standardization • E-business	• Market manipulation • Integrated reporting and informational access • Sarbanes Oxley • "Legislating Business Practices"

Figure 13.1—Regulatory Evolution

Furthermore, in a time of increasingly targeted punishment for institutions who fail to adhere to not the letter of the law, but the "*spirit of the law,*" we have witnessed some of the largest financial institutions pay outlandish fines since 2000. Even in this highly regulated industry, fines have risen from $332,700,000 in 2000 to over $4,187,000,000 in first five months of 2004[xxxi]. Additional industries on the threshold of unwanted review include insurance, pharmaceuticals, and of course, the constant scrutiny of technology firms. To add insult to injury, in late 2004 regulatory crusaders after the fact, say their efforts, actions, and laws may have created unnecessary turmoil—have they gone too far with an "overly-regulated" environment and how will they rectify the current compliance disarray? Regardless, we're years away from definitive answers and subsequent corrective proceedings.

As we can see, the regulatory climate has become more intimidating for businesses, and it has been a result of poorly managed firms in desperate need of purpose and realignment. The need and demand for rigorous regulations will become a significant catalyst for future realignment efforts. Consequently, a thorough innovative relevance practice must be promoted to assure the shareholders, employees, board members, and the general public that it is fair, equitable, and warranted to provide sustainable profits—that are legitimately earned profits! If you have your doubts, ask yourself where those fines come from? Why, in most cases, do firms that are caught with inferior regulatory controls and principles usually announce "restructurings" or realignments within 60 days?

Integration synergies

Because regulatory and realignment endeavors are treated as separate and distinct efforts, potential synergies between programs are missed, costing the organization in duplicate work, non-leveragability of investments, and siloed skills. If applicable realignment efforts are integrated with synergistically aligned regulatory needs, the cost to the organization can be minimized and the returns improved for both organizationally supported requirements.

Problems with compliance[xxxii] efforts typically reside with:

- They are difficult to understand and implement due to constantly changing and increasingly granular requirements,

- Compliance is viewed as a series of "one-offs," which are unrelated and seldom leveraged,

- Reporting and control is focused on a department-by-department level,

- Lack of consistency and capturing of data is leading to multiple "copies of the truth,"

- Information retrieval is time consuming and expensive,

- Compliance systems cannot meet stringent requirements needed for legal discovery and submission—lack of scrutiny,

- No enterprise examination of the complete picture—management is distracted by trying to run the business,

- Internal skill sets are few and stretched thin, and

- "Data Mart" proliferation coupled with new and untested internal controls.

When we examine these problems in the context of a realignment effort, we can realize several synergies. By leveraging the compliance informational repositories and solutions, we have a blueprint for assisting with accurate documentation sourcing and internal controls needed to guide our team's realignment repository (see Chapter 11).

Innovative realignments require appropriate controls. To be relevant and auditable, we need to provide records of decision making, adherence to local laws, and to provide for continuity of operations to meet SEC, NASD, or other industry requirements. Many corporations believe that compelling cases for realignment modifications are being mandated by regulators and their legal actions—a positive consequence of the legislative bills albeit expensive and disjointed. Experience has confirmed this to be true. Adoption demands unquestionable ethics, internal controls, and processes to manage the rapidly expanding legal regulations (see *Figure 13.2*).

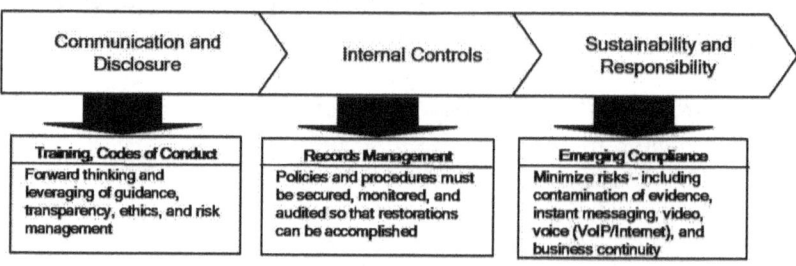

Figure 13.2—Satisfying Regulatory Requirements

The need for certainty, expectation management, and results compels not only financial markets, but our own realignment programs. By integrating relevant regulatory needs from the start, we can now be assured that we fulfill and potentially exceed the guidelines by collaboratively joining mandatory initiatives.

Communication and disclosure

If we examine *Figure 13.3*, we quickly gain a comprehensive level of urgency for the informational needs and communication requirements posed by some of the more well known legislative programs of recent memory. The disclosure of, conformance to and our compliance with, these regulations is what we have and continue to spend lavishly on during the last three years.

As corporations, we are struggling with the impediments of time, costs, overworked staffs, and even regulations that have deadlines, but little content. We strain against the axioms of:

- What does Sarbanes-Oxley really mean? The needs for internal controls that comply with new regulations are transforming enterprise risk management, so what should we do to reduce exposure?

- Nearly 30 percent of public companies are considering the discontinuance of earnings guidance. What qualitative, informational, and forecast information are being supplemented by these "non-guidance" firms?

- The spirit of the compliance requirements means more than putting a "check-in-a-box." Do we meet this?

- Legislation is just the beginning of things to come with an increase expected beyond prior regulations. What's next?

- New standards of accountability, integrity, and transparency are being mandated to restore investor confidence. Are we ready? What should we be anticipating?

- Have we reached a point where common sense is being legislated? How do we reach 100% compliance without putting our firm out-of-business?

- What measures must be undertaken to meet accelerated financial reporting deadlines and certification processes? Can we do it?

- Is the Audit committee overloaded with their struggle to cope with SXO (Sarbanes Oxley), the SEC, and listing requirements, in addition to their other responsibilities?

- Private shareholder and securities litigation have been unrelenting and are rapidly increasing. Are we vulnerable and can we continue to exist?

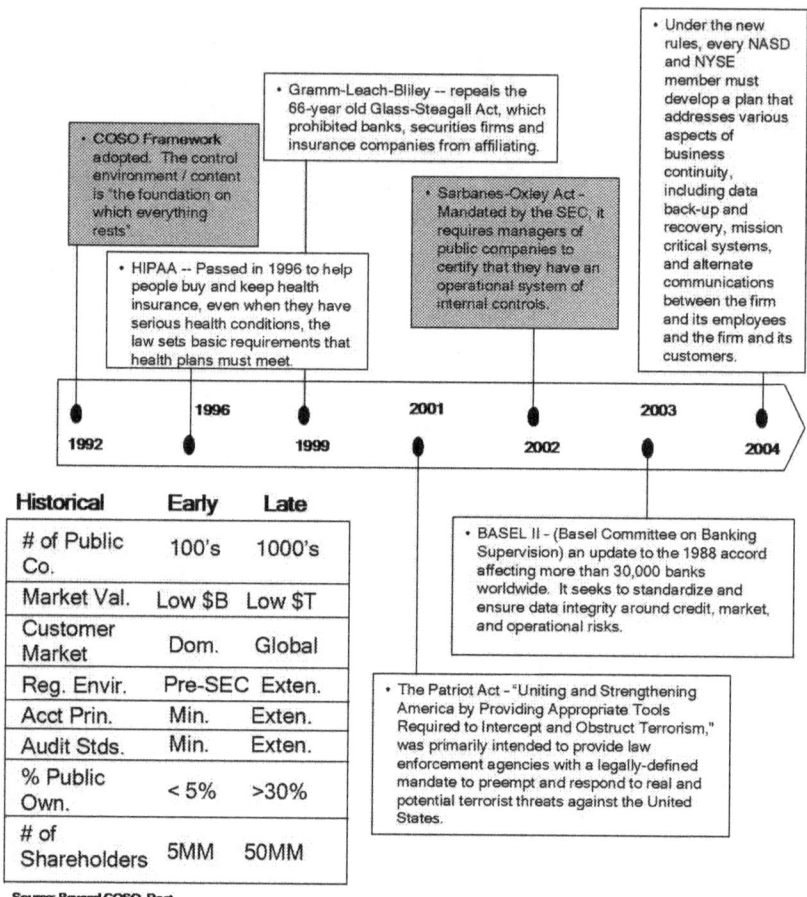

Figure 13.3—An Overview of Critical Legislation

The demands to satisfy and exceed regulations will be critical requirements for the iterative migration programs. Realignment efforts will require key compliance stakeholders who will need to be consulted and potentially approve critical decisions within the programs. As a result, suitable communications and disclosures must take place as part of the information and expectation management plans. Any training, education, and codes of conduct should be transmitted to the appropriate organizational departments and personnel before they are necessitated. Just like expectation management, the need for repeatability and adaptability are critical components of a superior compliance effort.

Failure to meet appropriate regulatory disclosures within realignment efforts can result in severe impediments including fines, sanctions, goodwill, personnel, partners, and market capitalization. The implications of any of the aforementioned can create financial turmoil for the short-term and operational viability in the long-term. To satisfy the needs of the current and projected regulatory requirements, compliance communications, and disclosures must meet or exceed published guidelines.

Internal controls

Internal controls to govern and guarantee conformity to regulations have become very familiar to executive offices with the adoption of Sarbanes-Oxley, new SEC requirements, and GAAP accounting procedures.

> Internal controls represent structured processes that ensure conformity to regulations, policies, and procedures, while offering repeatability, auditability, and recoverability. At a minimum, controls are designed to eliminate errors and/or variability within business systems, informational sources, personnel actions, and for commerce measurements.

The challenges for internal controls rest with a dynamic business environment, changing technologies, and outmoded methods of operations. Failures of internal controls needed for realignments include:

- Use of electronic records,

- Challenging business conditions,

- Complex environments—simple procedures,

- Crisis of e-mail,

- Faster response times required,

- Demand for greater content and breadth of informational sources,

- Exploding volumes,

- Mitigating legal risks and conducting due diligence,

- "Corporate Alzheimer's"—the inadvertent destruction of critical documents,

- Technological obsolescence,

- Preserving content with time,

- Structured and unstructured informational sources,

- Information accessibility—timeliness of information,

- Requirement for greater security and privacy controls, and

- Scarcity of needed resources.

Numerous internal controls were developed before the confidence of crisis that griped corporations and investors. While there have been significant strides in defining improvements for ensuring business-as-usual delivery, little progress has been made in assisting organizations with the capture of needed source and use documents contained within realignment programs.

Internal controls for realignment need to be tightly integrated with the informational sourcing storehouse discussed in Chapter 11. The E2EIM (End-to-End Informational Management) repository, combined with accurate internal controls, begins to automate the informational life-cycle needed to meet regulatory requirements while limiting legal liabilities. Controls ensure that as the information has passed its useful "life" and met the regulations, it is removed from the corporate storage vaults. E2EIM is not a product; it is a process that is integrated with the internal control requirements.

Conversely, sources of information should be destroyed to limit exposure, but only after they have been reviewed by legal experts. Destruction of documents can be a criminal offense (either intentionally or inadvertently), if they are still required or relevant to an existing or pending legal case. Internal controls help remove those impediments of short and long-term management, but they cannot eliminate the risks and needs for human intervention. When in doubt, seek expert advice for your industry, enterprise, and self regulating organization (if applicable). A word to the wise, don't think just because you are following "corporate policy" that you are immune from prosecution—ignorance of the law has never been an excuse.

Sustainability using E2EIM

The key to sustainability lies with a simple principle—realignment information has a life-cycle and it should be only warehoused as long as required by business and regulatory requirements. However, the traditional approaches and methods of informational source administration do not suffice for the complex relationships between and among structured and unstructured data. The usage of the E2EIM approach are being adopted to meet the needs of the innovative relevance leaders, while reducing operational risk, meeting regulatory needs, and improving realignment successes.

In spite of this, as with every quantum transformation with strategic and operational management controls, the reality of the situation is not keeping pace with the expectations of individuals and organizations who demand a quick yet simple solution to a very complex and growing problem.

The amalgamation and dissemination of information is not simply reserved for large enterprises. As evidenced from the evening news, it has become a mandate driven by shareholders, boards of directors, government regulators, and employees. As we have discussed, End-to-End Informational Management (E2EIM) is not just about managing stored sources—it concerns the use of data assets from "their cradle to their grave" within innovative relevance programs. While it is a complex issue, the benefits of achieving E2EIM are recognized as improving ROI, reducing operating costs (*i.e.*, TCO), increasing information availability, and promoting productivity of employees. Simply stated, E2EIM is about the process of the realignment information's life-cycle.

Achieving measurable and sustainable E2EIM results are hard work. The process starts with a clear appreciation of the sources and uses of the corporate information; its standardization, replication, migration, summarization, and integrity. Moreover, E2EIM is an emerging process-based solution set that mandates a strong business commitment, advanced planning, and a baselining of application characteristics. The challenges faced by organizations embracing E2EIM include:

- E2EIM requires management commitment outside of IT—driven by the business and not just on technical merits. An ability to sustain the initiative for the long-term requires full integration with the business and the IT plans. Failure to achieve accurate integration dooms the effort to be short-lived, unsustainable, and a financial liability.

- E2EIM involves a blending of initiatives and projects into a cohesive program of work. It cannot be approached as an ERP or CRM initiative, which consumes untold resources and several years of slow results. E2EIM is a series of steps that takes advantage of and is integrated with organizational initiatives such as compliance, business continuity, organizational process, and innovative relevance.

- E2EIM requires data cleansing and active management of information (*e.g.*, sources and uses). This area is one of the most underestimated and forgotten of E2EIM activities. While tremendous efforts and technologies have been deployed in this area, the failure to achieve a solid data foundation contributes significantly to E2EIM difficulties. Data cleansing must take place at a minimum within operational systems, data warehouses, and selected archival information used for compliance reporting and tracking.

By its very nature, E2EIM is not static. It is a layered and integrated series of controls, processes, and technology that can result in drastically improved information availability, usage, and bottom-line results for innovative programs. Many companies's today are unwittingly practicing E2EIM as an adjunct to their realignment efforts—using inefficient manual processes and fragmented technological products. A viable solution for organizational profitability, cost containment, and risk mitigation is contained within the E2EIM architecture.

By combining E2EIM with suitable internal controls, the communication and adherence to regulatory requirements that affect realignment programs can become straightforward and methodical. Failure to account for and integrate regulations will materially impede the initiatives and result in their potential failure or rollback.

Lessons learned

Regulatory compliance can be a critical asset in a well-planned realignment effort, or a severe limiting factor for those programs who fail to account for bureaucratic requirements. Regulatory challenges should not be considered an afterthought for innovative relevance programs and processes. Their needs must be met as part of the goals and objectives of the realignment, while promoting the inclusion of accurate policies and procedures for sustainability.

- Punishments for non-compliant activities are increasing, and the burden of proof is on the realignment teams to demonstrate they meet the requirements.
- Compliance is no longer about meeting the letter of the law, but the "spirit" of the regulation.

- With highly publicized failures since 2000, the need for stringent informational controls and irrefutability of data sources (structured and unstructured) must be met. You cannot wait until due diligence efforts are underway to address the requirements and constraints facing the organization—it is too late.

- Realignment efforts will highlight and worsen already deficient informational compliance capabilities.

- If properly planned, realignment efforts can moderate the overall expenses, and duplication of efforts common with one-off organizational regulatory compliance programs.

- Communication and disclosure require forward thinking and leverage of processes to promote transparency, risk aversion, and organizational acceptance.

- Records management, as part of the E2EIM, will be required for the automation of policies and procedures by providing a secure, monitored, and audited repository of compliance information.

- All manual and automated solutions will necessitate adaptability to meet the emerging compliance and regulatory needs driven by new technologies, self regulating organizations (SRO's), government agencies, and trade groups.

Chapter 14

Day-to-Day Must Remain Viable

Continuity of operations and customer experiences cannot be left to someone else

Our customers have become conditioned by online usage and immediate results in our orders, banking, and even social interactions. Their intolerance for interruptions and outages are shaped by highly available technology, and a perception that problems always "happen to the other person." When outages occur, they seek someone to blame. In most cases, the customer searches for another supplier or vendor to meet their needs in a timely, consistent, and flawless fashion. For customers, high availability and uniformity is a requirement—not an option. Their sympathy for the corporate realignment difficulties and operational interruptions are very low.

With the implementation of realignment changes comes uncertainty. This insecurity can create shifts in personnel, customer expectations, production delays, and even disruption of services or schedules. A cornerstone of all successful innovative relevance transformations is that, as new processes, procedures, or technologies are introduced, the current operational environments are maintained (as required until phase-out) to ensure customer satisfaction, product quality, and revenue generation.

The levels of performance within the product and service channels cannot be interrupted as a sacrifice to realignment goals and objectives. Consistency of operational delivery must be maintained. Any transition action or event must be non-disruptive to provide the foundational validation of realignment team activities and program plans. This reliability is ensured with adherence to operational and consumer standards, definitive processes, and repeatable delivery models in three critical areas (see *Figure 14.1*); service consistency, customer contact, and business continuance. For these reasons, transitional migration activities must be defined and tested as part of the corresponding realignment program. This testing provides the necessary certainty and sustainability within these interconnected remediation silos.

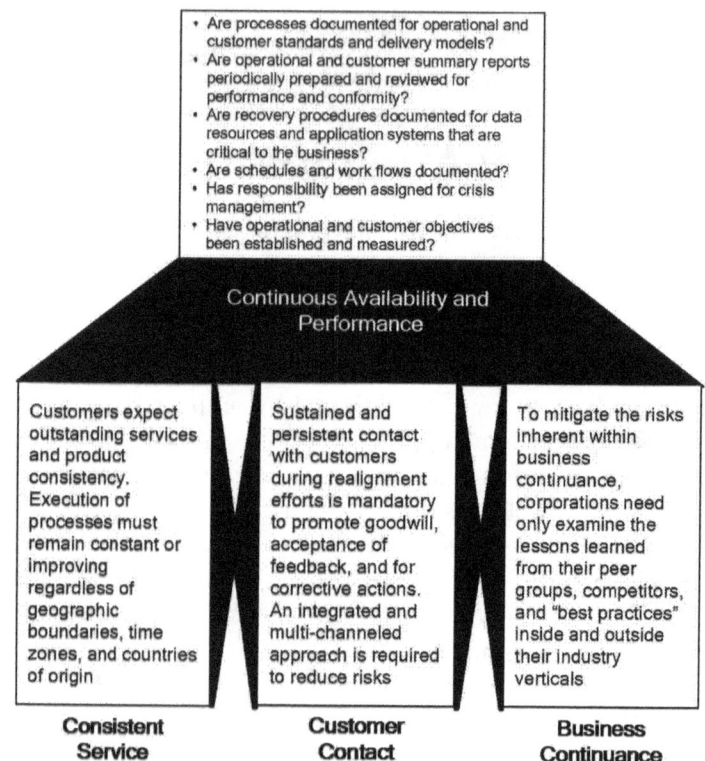

Figure 14.1—Managing Impediments of Day-to-Day

For corporations, the question is what should we do? In an environment of escalating litigation towards companies, what level of action and testing will diminish the risk of disruptions? Are there proven models that can be used to remove the uncertainty surrounding transformation viability as we move from the outmoded "As-Is' environment to a "To-Be" projection? Continuous availability is the best approach for corporate viability, as it integrates the practices of constant delivery into the critical assumptions for all realignment programs.

In this chapter, we will examine the potential operational and customer impediments to success, which must be aggressively controlled to obtain the realignment's vision, principles, goals, and objectives set forth. Failure can be quick for all innovative initiatives, when just one of them materially affects the day-to-day operational ability and qualities of the organization.

Consistent service models

Service and product consistency starts with comprehensive delineation and acceptance of roles and responsibilities within the delivery processes. With the completion of the baseline, the rigor and discipline of the "As-Is" artifacts establish the foundational condition of the day-to-day models. If these models are of inferior quality and ill-conceived, then additional steps to shore up the current environment will be required, while performing the realignment (to achieve the new models). These additional steps provide the "stepping stones" to aid with transition efforts. They also promote superior measurements and standards that will be adopted as part of the upcoming testing and conversion to the "To-Be" environment.

The existence or establishment of "standards of performance" will also clarify who has the responsibility for delivery, timings for completion, and adherence to quality management system[xxxiii] specifications (*i.e.,* conformity to a process within a production sequence). As we can see in *Figure 14.2*, the interdependencies and informational flows between the subordinate-processes will supply the consistency needed for day-to-day support of the operational and customer requirements.

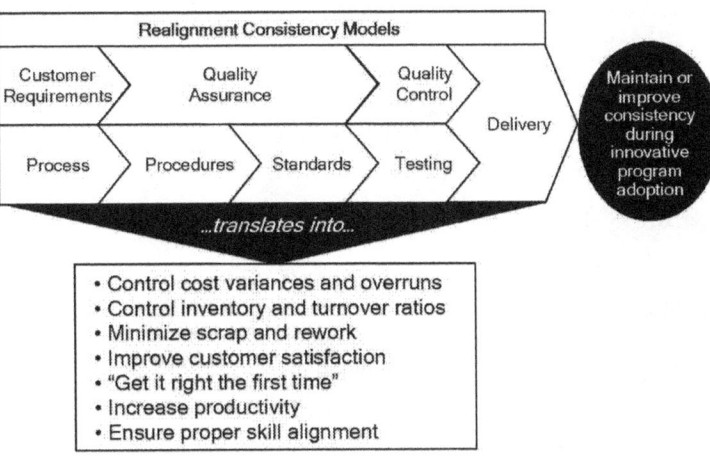

Figure 14.2—Service Model Convergence

The stability of delivery models must be guaranteed for any realignment effort to reach critical support and sustainability. The granular standards and procedures need to be tested with their new realignment program requirements before any downstream products or customers witness the end results. A simple example of a realignment, to take advantage of new business processes considered necessary for a merged entity in 2004, failed to account for on-going customer production and delivery requirements. It has cost the corporation over $400 million in top-line revenue, negative goodwill, and lost market share. It dominated their discussions with financial analyst's for over a year.

Customer contact

At the start of the millennium, when we examined the delivery of Internet services to our customers, we focused solely on providing information, product descriptions, and points of contact. Since then, a great many advancements in Internet technology have been realized. Still, these advancements have not resulted in a distinguishing advantage when conducting realignment programs. For a majority of realignment efforts, the focus concentrates on the end-state rather than the need for exceptional delivery during the risk-laden transitory periods.

Consequently, the incremental technology adoptions to mollify customer contact impediments have instead been implemented in "siloed" efforts with little forethought of integration—they have been applied as a "band-aid." The result of individual programs driving contact solutions, and the call centers performing related but separate campaigns and follow-ups, while potentially satisfying:

1. An immediate business crisis,

2. A reduction in communication costs, and

3. An improvement in campaign strategies,

have not materially benefited the customer nor improved levels of profitability required for the realignment's transitionary stages.

The solutions and mediums that must be integrated together for customer collaboration during our realignment efforts includes; the Internet, corporate servers, VoIP call center technologies, traditional technologies, and a host of configurable software (see *Figure 14.3*). Process and the supporting software are the keys for effective integration, and the future of innovative relevance programs. Recently, multiple onshore and offshore organizations have begun to aggressively adopt and implement these end-to-end solutions to help organizations with realignment transitions, while maintaining superior services and communications.

If we scrutinize the fundamental organizational drivers for adoption of old and new processes, to guarantee continuous product availability and organizational performance, while leveraging the technological infrastructures, we arrive at six tenets:

1. Improve or replace revenue generation during the implementation of new products or services—*i.e.*, enhance profits.

2. Increase and expand customer satisfaction, while minimizing schedule and production disruptions.

3. Enhanced channel points to provide multiple paths for consumer access, comments, and complaints.

4. Achieving cost reductions and/or avoidances—"book" short-term gains when practical.

5. Leveraging of capital assets and existing skill sets.

6. Provide flexible customer relationships that offer individualized services.

Yet, the underlying thought processes needed for successful realization of these tenets has gone unfulfilled. We have adopted a host of new solutions, even during the recent technology downturn, but their contribution to bottom line results and marketshare have not materialized. It is only with a comprehensive realignment approach, that embraces the diversity of customer service channels, can we obtain sustained and repeatable results.

Further fueling this rapid transition to integrated web and call center services, are the international organizations (including domestic operations with offshore presence), which are beginning to dominate the markets. They are accomplishing this ascendancy with cheap labor and easy access to advanced, global communication infrastructures. These established organizations are also very experienced with dialect training to ensure your customer receives clear, concise, and consistent personal exchanges.

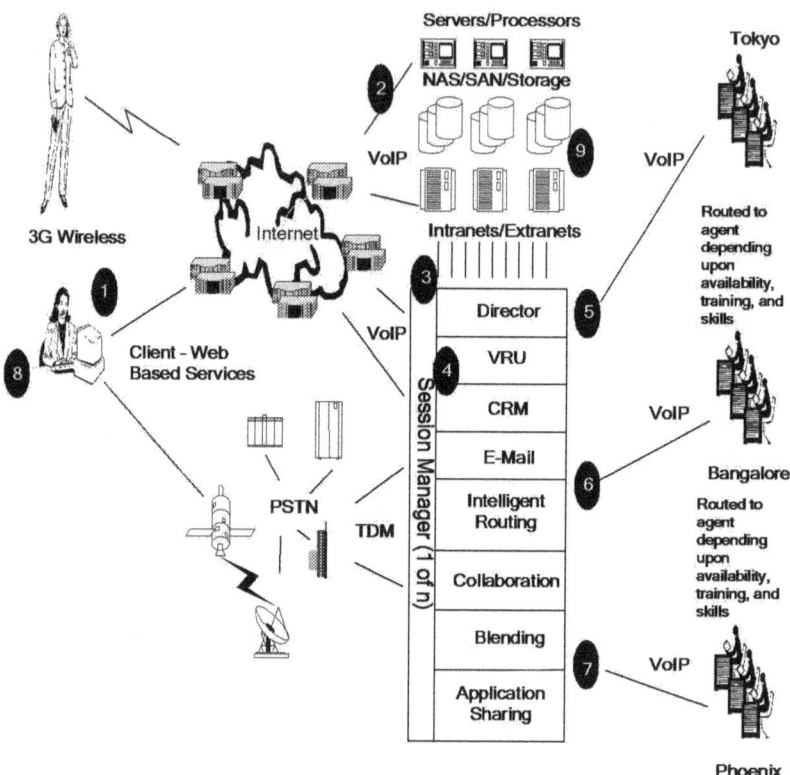

Figure 14.3—Details of a Contact Center

Many large organizations have already begun taking advantage of these collaborative and integrated solutions. By the same token, offshore organizations and outsourcers now can offer mid to small size organizations a chance to adopt new technologies and functionalities for their customers, while at the same time reducing costs.

Business continuance in uncertain times

You've just begun your second month of program execution, when a call is received at 3:57 a.m. into the main customer contact center—"your operations and call center environments, all locations, have been contaminated with a biological agent placed within the air filtration units." The immediate thoughts focus on the internal personnel who are present in these facilities. A secondary thought, once the personnel are secured, is can we recover? Have we or anyone else, ever been forced to deal with a multiple pronged attacks on our business facilities? Business viability is no longer about a natural disaster; it is about unplanned, crippling events that can strike at multiple locations simultaneously and without warning. Operational consistency must be proactively addressed as part of the innovative realignment efforts. An implied axiom of all realignment efforts requires that all programs plan for continuous operations.

Given this backdrop of uncertainty and unprecedented risks, our attention on business continuity has been heightened. Nonetheless, have we made progress, or are these expectations out of alignment with our innovative relevance programs? As organizational leaders, we need to ask our staff and ourselves these and other foundational questions, before we can be assured of the viability of our business continuity plans.

To complicate matters, since the start of the decade, thousands of new federal, state, and local compliance and regulatory requirements have been adopted. Furthermore, we have witnessed the unthinkable—the destruction of the free-enterprise physical icons that were at the core of a capitalistic society. However on average, less than 60% of North American firms plan to purchase additional business continuity (BC) services or equipment. Is the remainder of companies that confident in their ability, even in the face of global, internal, and financial turbulence?

Inside the United States' once unshakable worldwide leadership in technology, organizations have observed a loss of over two million jobs in the last five years, with a projection of another 500,000 being lost due to offshore competition by 2006. Additionally, as corporate profits continue to be squeezed by a sluggish economy, the budgets for information technology (IT) spending are now expected to only "swell" less than 2% on average for the next several years. Since 2000, this meager expansion represents over 45% of the total year-to-year increases.

Given the rapid pace of technology deployment, the disparate nature of large corporate systems, and the reliance on network infrastructure in today's IT architectures, yesterday's business continuance strategies will not hold up to today's rapid business recovery requirements.

Many large public firms express a remarkable confidence in their corporation's ability to resume operations during an unplanned interruption of their primary processing centers (*e.g.*, data centers, call centers, NOC's). These executives speak of their significant investments in infrastructure, personnel, and processes, which they have heavily automated since the mid-1990's. These assets have historically improved the corporation's productivity and position within world markets, while reducing their need on geographically dispersed personnel, equipment, and non-integrated vertical silos of delivery.

This confidence is unshaken even with the new millenniums' management mantras of "more with less," realignment, mergers, cost containment, synergies, and acquisitions. As the availability of skilled personnel decreases, corporate morale does as well. The expectation for rapid business continuity recovery appears to be increasing with executives—not decreasing. As the amount of information contained within a data center expands, at an average compounded rate of 16% per year (a highly conservative estimate), the time required recovering information from tape or offsite media can be expected to increase non-linearly.

These discrete findings point to several fundamental implications that have been unrecognized, directly or indirectly, as a result of business and global events (see *Figure 14.4*). First, the communication of objective capabilities for business continuance is not being presented to corporate decision makers and risk officers. This lack of realization and capabilities are creating liabilities, which shareholders and board members will not tolerate. As government and regulatory requirements are tightened and expanded, these operational risks that are not being actively managed, can spell disaster not only for the company, but also individually for each and every officer of the organization.

Secondly, business continuance cannot be approached in a vacuum. It requires substantial organizational involvement from all levels to ensure that a "fortress" delivery representation is in alignment with the limits of acceptable risk by the company, by the industry, and by the regulations. Business continuance must be championed at the executive ranks, and supported with enough purchasing authority to meet the financial goals and risk limits set forth by the Chief Risk Officer (CRO). It should not be viewed like an insurance policy, but as an integral part of the standard operating principles (SOP) needed to exceed realignment revenue, profit, and cost expectations.

Lastly, as a result of haphazard business and global transformations, significant negative consequences have been inflicted on many of the organization's remaining personnel. These anxieties and experiences, coupled with a stagnant economy, have pushed some employees to their physical and mental limits. In a disaster or unplanned outage situation, can we fully expect everyone to be available, when they have their own families and property to secure? We must plan for and test our business continuity operations with a diverse set of individuals to mitigate the risks and "non-planned" events. Who will be holding us liable if we fail to allocate activities to alleviate these potential impediments? Can we complete our realignment, or will it be only marginally successful? With our "tiered" outsourcing arrangements, can we count on them to perform to the same standards of superiority that we hold our employees? Has all this been tested, confirmed, and adjusted to reflect recent changes in our business procedures?

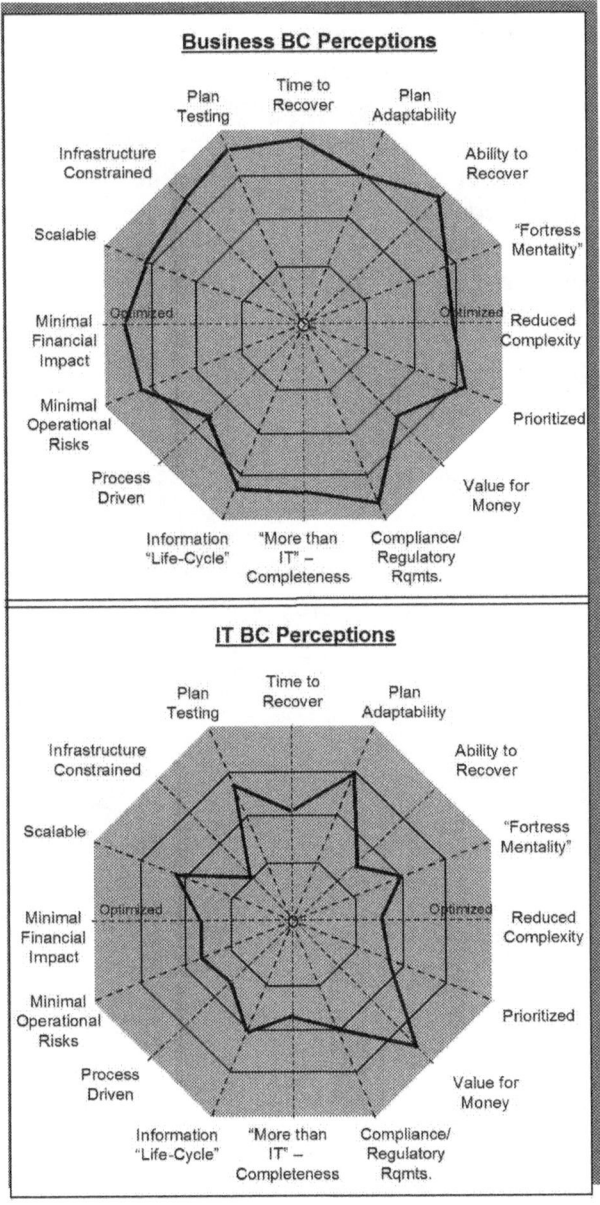

Figures 14.4—Perceptions are out of Alignment with Reality

The multi-billion dollar continuance question is, "when you lose your ability to meet the continuity of operations demanded by your customers, board, and regulators," is it a direct result of an uncontrollable business climate, or a lack of focus on the survivability of the organization? Business continuance is not about a paper process that can be dusted off when a critical situation occurs. It cannot be a paper fortress that lacks the day-to-day integration with existing processes, risks, practices, and personnel. Business continuance is about continuous availability, and avoiding the uncertainty and risk of recovery within realignment programs. Neither wealth nor power can potentially save a business or IT personnel from the inevitable, once business continuity efforts have failed—*responsibility*. For a realignment leader, when responsibility of business continuance is not met, liability is always what comes into question next.

Lessons learned

- Customer feedback and contacts must be adaptable as the realignment progresses.

- Business continuance cannot be left to chance—it must be actively tested and integrated into the transformation steps.

- Service consistency requires outstanding delivery and adherence to standards.

- Continuous availability is the cornerstone of all successful innovative relevance programs.

- Complacency must be identified and eliminated.

Chapter 15

The Seven Deadly Impediments
Recognize the behaviors before retribution is reached

Realignment impediments can take many forms and have different consequences depending upon the organizational personnel and culture (as discussed in Chapter 12). In some cases, personnel and cultures are unable to assimilate the rapid advancements in processes, quality, delivery schedules, or technology demanded by the iterative realignment programs. The change is just too great.

The focus of this chapter is concentrated the seven primary impediments to realignment programs posed by organizational cultures and personnel. These models need to be recognized for their characteristics, and their effects on the innovative relevance initiatives. If left unconstrained, they will create significant delays, disruptions, and loss of support for the program teams and sponsors.

"Let's make sure it fails..."

This model is usually associated with personnel who have hostility towards the realignment efforts. They may be openly aggressive or adversarial towards the need for innovative relevance within the organization, or it may manifest itself towards a specific team or member. These individuals can also exhibit passive-aggressive traits in making the programs fail by knowingly providing false or misleading information, unresponsive to artifact sourcing needs, or working the corporate "grapevine" to spread rumors and conjectures.

Personnel in this impediment classification should be dealt with swiftly and significantly. While a given amount of dialogue and challenging is typical and healthy for realignment programs, there are actions and behaviors that cannot be tolerated, if the realignment programs are expected to succeed within the established criteria. Realignment efforts that are taking place under the auspices of restructuring needs or mergers and acquisitions, usually experience a greater probability of this behavior than organizations innovating for competitive pressures or profits.

Unfortunately, the reaction taken to deal with staff seeking to undermine the realignment efforts will vary by the value the person represents towards the program. This dichotomy can be attributed to the need of a unique skill, prior experiences, industry knowledge, or operational processes possessed by the individual. In spite of this, the need to carry an obviously hostile employee or organizational element (*i.e.,* a small group) is short-lived. This is due to the obtainment of the "To-Be" state. As the new processes and models are adopted, the relative importance of these individuals diminishes. The organization only needs to embark upon its plans, while methodically isolating and phasing out these individuals as appropriate.

If staffing elimination is not in the organizational culture (see Chapter 8), then the organization should embark upon a 30-, 60-, or 90-day performance improvement plans for these personnel. Regardless of the actions taken, you cannot fail to respond. The person or group must be isolated, and the team needs to devise appropriate mitigation and control strategies to deal with the increase in program and realignment risks. Remember, don't overreact—just deal with it.

"My priority is greater than yours...!"

This impediment is very common in income and competitively directed realignment programs. Individuals and teams sometimes lose sight of the larger goals in favor of making themselves influential. The drivers for these behavioral issues can be strong career aspirations, non-team player (an internal politician), strong self-importance or worth, and distain for the managers within and among the programs. Team and individual actions will manifest themselves as:

- Status known by sponsors or senior executives before being reported to the realignment leaders or managers,

- Lack of information sharing among the realignment team,

- Teams that create an abnormal number of open issues on other program groups,

- Continual submission of project scope enhancements that cross into other program boundaries and deliverables,

- Excessive publication of results—over distribution of progress, status, and importance,

- Constant requests for special treatments and benefits, and

- Delivery is met once they determine "what's in it for me?"

While these types of personnel usually are good performers, the amount of control and management oversight can be time consuming and tedious. Staff or groups that adopt these impediments necessitate that they are held tightly to schedules, deliverables, program scopes, and objectives. Furthermore, their actions warrant the creation of measurable program criteria tied to their quarterly or annual performance to ensure they understand how their actions and behaviors will materially affect their employee rating, reimbursements, or merit increases. Individuals in this category understand any action that negatively reflects on their performance. Bring it to their attention!

"On the first blue moon…"

Regardless on the drivers for the realignment programs, an organization will experience impediments that fall into this classification. Unlike other categories where staff may exhibit dysfunctionality, but are still individual contributors, personnel in this classification tend to be non-aggressive and reluctant participants. Obstructions can be caused by feeling passed over for critical roles, a belief that the organization has continually failed to recognize their skills, or even an impression that they are being "shunned" or not consulted.

Consequently, their actions are always being called into question. Their delivery is late, they fail to properly report status, and they do not highlight issues until someone calls them into question. Usually, they are always preparing or presenting some reason for their inadequate performance against the programs' success criteria.

Nevertheless, depending upon the circumstances, these personnel can be quickly transformed into valuable contributors. They have the required foundation and abilities, but they never seem to use it. With suitable guidance and support, these individuals cannot only reduce the delivery impediments, but they can be outstanding success stories for the realignment labors. For a small team, it is their attitude that needs transformation.

The sustaining solution for this impediment resides with the individual. Careful work must be performed with the program leader and human resources (HR) department. If they are an outside contractor, making a switch or adjustment is simpler. If they are an employee, evaluate their history with HR and then make an objective decision. Let the facts speak for themselves.

"So you want me to deliver...?"

 While not a common impediment within time sensitive innovative relevance realignments, it still can be encountered. Usually found within geographically separated groups or individuals who are away from the dynamics and interactions of the realignment team leaders. Characterized by a lack of purpose or urgency, the results are the fist indicators of problems—there are little or no results!

The cause of these impediments is wide ranging. Experience has shown that individuals or groups lack appreciation for their programs' importance, believing that their efforts are autonomous and do not impact others, or have been assigned low priorities to the program needs and actions (*i.e.,* they have other "higher" priorities). The challenge when this impediment is diagnosed is that it can reformulate itself quickly into one of the other six classifications before the real problems are uncovered.

For example, the realignment sponsor and leader may attribute the lack of progress as a "cultural difference", a "misunderstanding", or an "aberration." Consequently, these individuals or groups are given a second chance to meet the program criteria and actions. The fundamental problem could be a passive-aggressive impediment (*i.e.,* "Let's make it Fail") or even a belief that this is the wrong effort and they are not going to waste the organizational resources (*i.e.,* "It's not my Fault!").

Impediments in this classification require the realignment leader and sponsor to put individuals on very "short-leashes." Time tables will need to be accelerated to make up for lost time, reporting and tracking requirements will be more frequent, and validation of progress must be made actively (I'm from the "Show Me' state).

"It's a technological marvel...!"

We've all experienced this impediment. We have witnessed programs or realignment efforts lost in the implementation of a technological component.

Months go by, millions are spent, and yet the results are not even close to those projected or expected. Nevertheless, the team or individuals who are implementing this technology continue to express an unwavering steadfastness to profits, results, or productivity benefits. In these cases, the technology and the people promoting it have become obstacles. It is technology for the sake of technology. Let's look at a case study of one such event.

John, 44, was part of a large services organization; ZYX Services[xxxiv]. He had been with the organization nearly four years, and was looking towards a long and productive career with ZYX Services. He was a manager within the information technology (IT) organization, and was responsible for application development.

John and his team were working on the delivery of a new application. This new application was going to utilize the "latest" technologies. He and his team had spent many months preparing for the use of this new application; training, educating, prototyping, and performing simulations. They were one month away from implementation and roll-out to the business units. He and the team were confident that their new application was going to be accepted by the business users, who were just beginning this week to test the new application system. However as the testing progressed, it was obvious that while the new application used the latest technologies, it did not provide the solution required by the business unit in support of the realignment efforts. The business requirements and drivers for the creation of the application had gone unfulfilled—lost in a haze of technical jargon.

On Friday of the second week of user testing, John was asked by the realignment team leader to not only explain the discrepancies, but to also figure out the costs of the "rework" to make the application perform as required. At this time, the application would not be implemented because it did not meet the business user requirements. A working meeting was set for Thursday of next week to discuss the development process, and the alternatives for correcting the application. John prepared his "rebuttal," costs, and alternatives. On Thursday, all involved parties met to discuss the sequence of events that had caused this development application to be unsuccessful.

As the meeting progressed, it became apparent that the business requirements had been gradually lost to the fervor of implementing new technologies. Realignment requirements and drivers where replaced with technology drivers and non-business goals. The costs to make the application work as required were in excess of the initial cost of its original development. John and his project team had failed to understand the rationale for the realignment program. In addition, the application lacked technological consistency, was overly complex, and was not integrated with ZYX Services other applications.

As a result of this meeting, it was determined that the project would be canceled. John's lack of comprehension of the realignment program's importance directly influenced his chances of promotion and advancement. John was subsequently promoted "downward," and left the company two years later. Several months after the program was "shelved," the application was redeveloped (as the fundamental drivers did not go away) under a non-IT manager using the realignment's objectives (without using the "latest" technologies). In spite of this, the cost and delay of this "redevelopment" allowed their competitors to enter the market segment six months before ZYX's activities were completed.

It's a familiar, but real event. If the program had utilized an iterative approach, as discussed in Chapter 7, the impediments may not have materialized. The unshakable belief that technology is "good," regardless of the realignment need, is false. Technology must only be used if it is justified and contributes to the on-going profits of the realignment initiatives.

"But it meets my demand…"

Program teams or members with an inordinate desire to consume more resources than required, are significant risks for the realignment sponsor. These excesses can generate substantial costs, and reduce the overall profitability measures set forth by the realignment. While we tend to think of scope increases consuming more and more resources, this can also be evidenced in excessive plan contingencies and outside service requests.

Further characteristics of this impediment can be seen with teams' concentrating their efforts into a "pet" process or "preferred" division. Holistically, the program unnecessarily "slights" other critical departments or groups in favor of another. The program team or individual ensures that the benefits meets the business unit first and the realignment program goals and measures second.

Program teams in this classification will usually meet the overall needs of the realignment effort. Although, like some government bills and laws, there are other hidden agendas that are being satisfied which have little to do with the realignment activities and objectives. Problems are usually uncovered when one of these items restricts or inhibits the realignment's success criteria.

Impediments in this area can be moderated using:

- Peer reviews between teams,
- Structured reviews of deliverables and progress,
- Granular tracking of expenses and time reporting,
- Cost accounting and allocation of capitalized resources,
- Continual review of outside services,
- Procurement scrutiny of vendor purchases,
- Reduction in discretionary dollar purchases to eliminate the "nickel-and-diming" of capital or services, and
- Improved reporting to track charges with stringent reviews covering chargebacks, allocations, budgets, expenses, actuals, and forecasts.

Personnel found making use of this impediment should be counseled. Depending upon the severity, items should be noted within their personnel files and mandatory education should be undertaken. In the most severe cases, immediate termination may be warranted.

"It's not my fault...!"

We all know of individuals who use this impediment as an excuse for habitually poor performance. While this is not an impediment when the realignment programs are meeting deadlines and performance objectives, it can be a significant personnel management issue when an individual or set of programs are under-delivering. Behavioral dysfunctionality during these circumstances becomes discernible  with spikes in employee "probations," performance improvement plans, issue logging, blaming of others openly, excessive e-mailing, and status reports targeting groups or individuals by name (rather than the problem). Impediments in this area become personal attacks for those playing the "blame game."

As in other impediment mitigation strategies, counseling should be the first choice. Many times, the individual lacks the appropriate management and communication skills for team leadership or interaction. While this is not an overnight success, it is easily correctable. Realignment leaders need to watch for the signs of this impediment. Correct actions early—or risk conditioning others that this behavior is tolerated. It can spread quickly forcing sponsors and leaders away from the goals and deliverables of the programs for extended periods of time. It left unchecked, it creates an unhealthy team environment.

If you have a multi-cultural team that has not worked together previously, this behavior can be unrecoverable. In cultures that are conflict adverse or hierarchically based, individuals will accept the criticism with little response. They will endure the blame while planning their exit. The loss of talent and critical personnel for the realignment programs will be seen as a failure for the initiatives.

Lessons learned

The characterizing of impediment models is useful for identification and corrective action by the realignment leaders. While each model has unique attributes, it is important to realize their commonalities.

- Once identified, each case must be documented and placed within the informational sources (*i.e.*, E2EIM) of the realignment effort.

- Any staff action must be based on objective information, which results in requirements, actions, or adjustments, with definitive timeframes and success criteria.

- Impediments cannot be left unchecked. Action must be immediate and applied consistently across all programs. No exceptions.

- People will behave like people. Expect dysfunctionality in times of change and don't be surprised or overreact.

- Sometimes several impediments can be acting or on-going within a single group. Look for the root cause and prepare action plans to address the source—not the circumstance!

Chapter 16

"...A Flea in One's Ear..."

The organization will reap what it sows

You've understood the innovative relevance realignment fundamentals. Their meaning and intentions have been assimilated into your actions and operating philosophies. The sponsorship is clear, and the end-goals are in place.

We have witnessed that the obtainment of realignment efforts using innovative relevance techniques can be organizationally profitable, yet present a series of transformations and assumptions sequences, which must be continuously evaluated and measured. Furthermore, realignment efforts are achieved using iterative methods, as we cannot hope to transform the organization in one single, broad action. Even if we could achieve all our goals at one time, could we sustain them?

These principles are what guides and focuses your realignment efforts. They are the foundations for your success.

Crawl

As we explored in Chapters 1 to 4, there are prerequisites that we must meet before we can undertake any consideration of engaging in an innovative relevance set of programs. We need an unambiguous vision and principles tied to the end-state. Moreover, we have to lead with humility but be able to demonstrate exemplary ethics and integrity, while motivating our staffs and organizations during uncertain times.

Our own experience coupled with those of our teams, must create a balance of overlapping, yet complimentary skills. This robustness is required to complete not only the definition of the programs, but their eventual execution. As final preparation, we minimally require commitment from our direct organization, in addition to the extended family of alliance members, joint ventures, and critical suppliers.

Walk

With our preparation behind us, we have to concretely understand the current situational events within the organization. A baseline of performance measures, strengths, weaknesses, and suitability, must be collected and synthesized into a common model for analysis.

The baseline forms the anchor for an assessment and projection of our abilities as we look to the future. A future driven by new goals, measurable objectives, and operating policies. The "To-Be" model is the destination on our road map. The baseline is our starting point. The process of "driving" from the current location to the future destination is where our iterative realignment programs take place.

Iterative techniques are used to move our organization from a stopped or "crawling" position to a "faster mode of transportation." We'll start off slowly, getting "wins" behind our teams and taking advantage of short-term efforts, which can increase organizational commitment and solidify sustained support. Once in motion, the realignment efforts will accelerate providing profits and successful results.

Run

With the programs underway, active administration techniques and decisions will need to be quickly adopted (see Chapters 8 to 11). Like our farmer of earlier sections, we have planned for many activities once the crops have sprouted, but the crops first need to germinate. For our realignment efforts, the programs need to be defined, staffed, and prioritized, before we can invoke our disciplined reporting, tracking, and measuring devices.

As we discussed in Section 4, we need to actively mollify risks, impediments, and chaos within our realignment programs. There are techniques we must embrace to manage expectations, deal with regulatory compliance issues, and maintain our "As-Is" daily environments, while being diligent against the seven deadly impediments.

Succeed

Finally, we must learn from others and listen. The variability of choices and conditions that can arise within innovative relevance realignments does not afford sponsors and leaders to accept absolutes. Experience has taught us that flexibility, adaptability, and humility are assets.

When you have doubts or concerns, look outside your industry's' vertical and crossover into other domains. There are a great many lessons to be learned and problems avoided by starting where someone else left off. Remember, in innovative relevance realignments:

> *...it is not how much an individual knows that lets them succeed. It is how an individual uses what they know, and how they find out what they don't know that makes them successful...*

Appendices

A. Organizational Baseline and Assessment

Individual analysis will need to be completed for all departments and divisions with the corporation (regardless of profit or overhead classification). These should then be summarized/compiled into the supporting lines of businesses (LOB's).

1. Planning

With what frequency are the strategic plans reviewed against organizational results and directions? _____

With what measurability is there a documented planning process within the enterprise? `L 2 3 4 5 6 H`

    A.   Within a division? `L 2 3 4 5 6 H`

    B.   Within a department? `L 2 3 4 5 6 H`

    C.   By geography? `L 2 3 4 5 6 H`

To what measure do the plans reflect organizational activities and strategy? `L 2 3 4 5 6 H`

With what measurability do the plans include assumptions? `L 2 3 4 5 6 H`

    A.   Financial requirements? `L 2 3 4 5 6 H`

    B.   Milestones? `L 2 3 4 5 6 H`

    C.   Responsibilities? `L 2 3 4 5 6 H`

    D.   Objectives? `L 2 3 4 5 6 H`

    E.   Principles? `L 2 3 4 5 6 H`

With what efficacy does senior management utilize the plans to ensure applicability and consistency across departments and divisions? `L 2 3 4 5 6 H`

With what determinability are the business continuance plans incorporated into the planning cycle?

`L|2|3|4|5|6|H`

With what measurability is there a formalized planning process?

`L|2|3|4|5|6|H`

With what measurability are department or employee objectives and measures tied to the business plans?

`L|2|3|4|5|6|H`

With what measurability are capital requirements contained with the plans and tied to performance or achievements?

`L|2|3|4|5|6|H`

With what measurability are clear profitability objectives and thresholds incorporated within the plans?

`L|2|3|4|5|6|H`

With what measurability are comments or feedback from employees incorporated into the planning process?

`L|2|3|4|5|6|H`

With what quantifiability are the objectives measurable and meaningful for employees?

`L|2|3|4|5|6|H`

With what quantifiability will present or proposed litigation affect the obtainment of the measurable objectives?

`L|2|3|4|5|6|H`

With what measurability are the plans' objectives supported by direct measures that are tied to department or group levels?

`L|2|3|4|5|6|H`

With what measurability are employees assessed on their adherence to stated goals and objectives as part of their quarterly or annual performance evaluations?

`L|2|3|4|5|6|H`

With what measurability are staffing levels aligned with stated planning goals and measurements?

`L|2|3|4|5|6|H`

With what measurability are information technology resources allocated to support plan objectives and measures?

`L 2 3 4 5 6 H`

With what measurability are clearly defined policies aligned with the organizational goals and principles stated within the plans?

`L 2 3 4 5 6 H`

With what measurability are procedural sequences aligned with stated polices?

`L 2 3 4 5 6 H`

With what measurability are procedures adhered to by employees and staff as part of their daily activities?

`L 2 3 4 5 6 H`

With what measurability are volumes and activities captured to ensure conformity to plan assumptions and projected drivers?

`L 2 3 4 5 6 H`

With what adaptability are plans adjusted due to performance related successes or failures?

`L 2 3 4 5 6 H`

   A.   Objective adjustments?

`L 2 3 4 5 6 H`

   B.   Policy adjustments?

`L 2 3 4 5 6 H`

   C.   Procedural adjustments?

`L 2 3 4 5 6 H`

   D.   Principle adjustments?

`L 2 3 4 5 6 H`

   E.   Measurement corrections?

`L 2 3 4 5 6 H`

With what measurability are informational needs identified as part of the planning process?

`L 2 3 4 5 6 H`

With what measurability does the process provide adequate time and adjustments to be made as part of its development and refinement?

`L 2 3 4 5 6 H`

2. Policies and Structure

With what measurability are detailed operational
functions identified and documented?

`L 2 3 4 5 6 H`

With what measurability are proper supervision levels
maintained to meet the quality, ethical, and
operational targets?

`L 2 3 4 5 6 H`

With what measurability are functional groups
consolidated to ensure consistency while minimizing
rework?

`L 2 3 4 5 6 H`

With what measurability are communications
properly conducted to promote policy and procedural
acceptance and usage?

`L 2 3 4 5 6 H`

With what measurability does the organizational
structure reflect the actual functional activities within
the organization?

`L 2 3 4 5 6 H`

With what measurability do staffing roles and
responsibilities meet stated procedural or policy
requirements?

`L 2 3 4 5 6 H`

With what measurability are the policies self sufficient
without the organizational plan?

`L 2 3 4 5 6 H`

With what measurability are the procedures self
sufficient without the organizational plan?

`L 2 3 4 5 6 H`

With what measurability are policies and functional
alignment used to promote proper separation of duties
and check and balances?

`L 2 3 4 5 6 H`

With what quantifiability are policies and procedures
measured for their efficacy, efficiency, and
effectiveness?

`L 2 3 4 5 6 H`

With what quantifiability are departments or groups measured for their adherence to stated polices and procedures?

L	2	3	4	5	6	H

With what measurability do the policies and procedures support the organizational structure?

L	2	3	4	5	6	H

With what measurability are policies updated?

L	2	3	4	5	6	H

With what measurability are procedures updated to meet results and policy changes?

L	2	3	4	5	6	H

With what measurability are policies in place to support record retentions and regulatory requirements?

L	2	3	4	5	6	H

Is there a centralized informational repository where employees can access policies and procedures?

_____

Are employees trained in the rationale and implications of stated policies and procedures? often are these required for "refreshing"?

_____

Are automated employee education and training sessions available via a corporate Intranet? Are they successful? Do these match the reality of policy and procedural usage?

_____

3. Alliances and Joint Ventures

With what measurability are organizational alliances integrated with stated plans?

`L 2 3 4 5 6 H`

With what measurability to alliances and joint ventures support the operational requirements and guidelines stated within corporate goals and objectives?

`L 2 3 4 5 6 H`

With what measurability are external linkages reviewed for conformity to shared values, ethical standards, and organizational policies (i.e., to they adhere to the same behavior as our corporation)?

`L 2 3 4 5 6 H`

With what quantifiability does formalized processes exists to measure the effectiveness of alliances and joint ventures?

`L 2 3 4 5 6 H`

With what adaptability are changes made to existing relationships to reflect evolving results, perceptions, and channel needs?

`L 2 3 4 5 6 H`

With what measurability are there definitive relationship personnel assigned to each alliance or joint venture?

`L 2 3 4 5 6 H`

With what determinability to the recommendations of relationship personnel deemed to be objective and based upon actual results?

`L 2 3 4 5 6 H`

With what measurability are there statistically meaningful metrics to assess and project alliance and joint venture results?

`L 2 3 4 5 6 H`

With what measurability are results communicated to affected parties or stakeholders in order to secure their feedback?

`L 2 3 4 5 6 H`

With what measurability are comments and feedback incorporated into corrective actions outside of the stated policies and procedures?

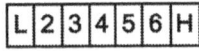

With what measurability is there a process to clearly identify, define, and create alliances and joint ventures?

Potential Planning and Organizational Artifacts

    A.   Operational plans

    B.   Strategic plans

    C.   Planning process

    D.   Corporate communications

    E.   Integration with budgeting cycles

    F.   Stakeholder interviews

    G.   Historical reports/plans

    H.   Plan to actual tracking and procedures

    I.   Measurements and metrics

    J.   Principles

    K.   Objectives

    L.   Planning disciplines

    M.   Mapping associations

    N.   Vision and shared values

    O.   Organizational charts

    P.   Branding strategies

    Q.   Channel distribution

    R.   Market analysis and plans

    S.   Competitive analysis

    T.   Planning repositories

    U.   Risk plans/mitigation strategies

B. Business Area Analysis

Individual analysis will need to be completed for all departments and divisions with the corporation (regardless of profit or overhead classification). These should then be summarized/compiled into the supporting lines of businesses (LOB's).

With what determinability are the business area's objectives and goals clearly defined?

`L 2 3 4 5 6 H`

With what determinability are there processes used by the business area for plan obtainment?

`L 2 3 4 5 6 H`

With what measurability are the goals and objectives adjusted based upon monthly or quarterly results?

`L 2 3 4 5 6 H`

With what quantifiability is information technology expenditures for the business are tied to the achievement of departmental or divisional objectives?

`L 2 3 4 5 6 H`

With what quantifiability are measures and metrics directly tied to the business area's performance?

`L 2 3 4 5 6 H`

With what efficacy are the metrics statistically significant for the forecasted or actual results?

`L 2 3 4 5 6 H`

With what quantifiability are service level agreements in direct support of the business area objectives?

`L 2 3 4 5 6 H`

With what measurability do business area teams approve capital or strategic purchases or investments tied to performance measurements?

`L 2 3 4 5 6 H`

With what determinability are discrete business area priorities set by the enterprise plans?

`L 2 3 4 5 6 H`

With what determinability are priorities communicated to personnel to demonstrate urgency and significance?

`L 2 3 4 5 6 H`

With what measurability are delivery conflicts resolved utilizing previously defined policies, procedures, and processes?

`L 2 3 4 5 6 H`

With what certainty do success criteria support the stated objectives?

`L 2 3 4 5 6 H`

    A.   By department?

`L 2 3 4 5 6 H`

    B.   By division?

`L 2 3 4 5 6 H`

    C.   By employee?

`L 2 3 4 5 6 H`

With what determinability do the product planning cycles accurately reflect results required by business area objectives?

`L 2 3 4 5 6 H`

With what determinability do the financial controls reflect effective measurements for required performance results?

`L 2 3 4 5 6 H`

With what certainty do business area personnel understand, accept, and support business area goals, objectives and performance criteria?

`L 2 3 4 5 6 H`

With what applicability are operational processes in direct support of business area goals (monthly, quarterly, and yearly)?

`L 2 3 4 5 6 H`

With what measurability is personnel feedback incorporated into delivery cycles? (Are they timely?)

`L 2 3 4 5 6 H`

With what applicability are business drivers changed due to evolving competitive pressures?

`L 2 3 4 5 6 H`

    A.   Industry changes?

`L 2 3 4 5 6 H`

    B.   Alliance changes?

`L 2 3 4 5 6 H`

C.   Economic changes?

`L|2|3|4|5|6|H`

D.   Personnel changes?

`L|2|3|4|5|6|H`

E.   Technology changes?

`L|2|3|4|5|6|H`

With what effectiveness are changes quickly
incorporated into operational plans?

`L|2|3|4|5|6|H`

With what probability are personnel adequately
trained on the performance objectives and the roles
their contribution makes in their achievement?

`L|2|3|4|5|6|H`

With what level of acceptability are department
decisions supported by senior management?

`L|2|3|4|5|6|H`

With what level of efficacy are individual personnel
performance criteria directly support business are
objectives? Enterprise objectives?

`L|2|3|4|5|6|H`

With what measurability do the approval and control
processes meet the needs of the department or
business area?

`L|2|3|4|5|6|H`

With what level of standardization do all departments
adhere to stated policies and procedures?

`L|2|3|4|5|6|H`

With what determinability are the needs of the
alliance members met by business area or
departmental actions?

`L|2|3|4|5|6|H`

With what determinability are the needs of the
customers met by business area or departmental
actions?

`L|2|3|4|5|6|H`

With what certainty to the business area quality
measurements meet the requirements of the
organization?

`L|2|3|4|5|6|H`

A. The needs of the customers?   `L|2|3|4|5|6|H`

B. The needs of the alliance members?   `L|2|3|4|5|6|H`

With what measurability are outside vendors or service provider needs unduly influencing the performance results?   `L|2|3|4|5|6|H`

With what measurability are quality standards being accurately captured and communicated to the organization? Are they consistent?   `L|2|3|4|5|6|H`

Are there defined corrective processes and procedures that can be invoked for immediate operational actions?   _____

With what certainty do business continuance efforts meet the needs of the business area or department?   `L|2|3|4|5|6|H`

With what level of granularity do the business continuance processes and procedures meet organizational needs?   `L|2|3|4|5|6|H`

To what certainty are there definitive owners of processes and procedures?   `L|2|3|4|5|6|H`

With what measurability are there defined roles and responsibilities for personnel that directly relate to their performance requirements?   `L|2|3|4|5|6|H`

With what measurability does the business area Intranet support the needs of the employee?   `L|2|3|4|5|6|H`

Potential Business Area Artifacts:

A. Budgets

B. Plans

C. Policies

D. Procedures

E.   Presentations

F.   Web sites/pages

G.   Dashboards

H.   Surveys

I.   Economic projections

J.   Production schedules

K.   Capital investments

L.   Consulting reports

M.   Audit reports

N.   Analysts presentations

O.   Monthly/Weekly reports

P.   Processes

Q.   Regulatory submissions

C. IT Environments

The use of the questions below must be tempered with relevant industry and operational constraints. Consequently, not all questions will be applicable. Artifact sourcing should be obtained for all questions proposed.

Does the organization have a published CIO agenda?   _____

Does the IT plans and objectives directly map to the organizational directions?   _____

With what certainty are the IT projects funded as a direct result of the organizational goals and objectives?   `L 2 3 4 5 6 H`

With what level of disparity are IT policies and procedures not in support of the organizational performance indicators?   `L 2 3 4 5 6 H`

With what certainty is the IT PMO tied directly into other organizational program offices?   `L 2 3 4 5 6 H`

With what maturity are IT processes using industry recognized models for:

    A.   Applications?   `L 2 3 4 5 6 H`

    B.   Network management?   `L 2 3 4 5 6 H`

    C.   System Support?   `L 2 3 4 5 6 H`

    D.   Maintenance?   `L 2 3 4 5 6 H`

    E.   Problems/fixes?   `L 2 3 4 5 6 H`

    F.   Issue management?   `L 2 3 4 5 6 H`

    G.   Scope control?   `L 2 3 4 5 6 H`

H.   Allocation and chargeback?   `L 2 3 4 5 6 H`

I.   Training?   `L 2 3 4 5 6 H`

J.   Education?   `L 2 3 4 5 6 H`

K.   Technology refreshing?   `L 2 3 4 5 6 H`

L.   Web servicing?   `L 2 3 4 5 6 H`

M.   Customer contact?   `L 2 3 4 5 6 H`

N.   Call center?   `L 2 3 4 5 6 H`

O.   Regulatory management?   `L 2 3 4 5 6 H`

P.   Information life-cycle (ILM)?   `L 2 3 4 5 6 H`

Q.   Requirements definition?   `L 2 3 4 5 6 H`

R.   Outsourcing?   `L 2 3 4 5 6 H`

S.   Offshore?   `L 2 3 4 5 6 H`

T.   Controls?   `L 2 3 4 5 6 H`

U.   Operations   `L 2 3 4 5 6 H`

V.   Reporting   `L 2 3 4 5 6 H`

W.   Business intelligence?   `L 2 3 4 5 6 H`

X.   Competitive analytics?   `L 2 3 4 5 6 H`

Y.   Benchmarking?   `L 2 3 4 5 6 H`

Z.   Process management?   `L 2 3 4 5 6 H`

AA. Six Sigma?   `L 2 3 4 5 6 H`

BB. Business process outsourcing?   `L 2 3 4 5 6 H`

CC. Business continuance?   `L 2 3 4 5 6 H`

DD. Continuous availability?   `L 2 3 4 5 6 H`

(with each of the above, artifacts should be obtained and categorized including contracts)

What are the expenditures for IT?   _____

    A.   As a percentage of sales?   _____

    B.   As a percentage of profits?   _____

    C.   What are the returns on investments?   _____

    D.   Personnel?   _____

    E.   Equipment?   _____

    F.   Maintenance?   _____

    G.   Capital?   _____

    H.   Administration?   _____

    I.   Training?   _____

    J.   Recruiting?   _____

    K.   Outside services?   _____

    L.   Discretionary?   _____

    M.   "Write-offs" or "Write-downs?"   _____

N.   "Capitalized" software or programs?   _____

(with each of the above, artifacts should be obtained and categorized including contracts)

With what measurability are the volumes of applications and systems tracked?

`L 2 3 4 5 6 H`

With what applicability are the volumes and measurements consistent with the business value achieved with their deployment?

`L 2 3 4 5 6 H`

With what consistency are applications ranked by their cost to benefit contributions?

`L 2 3 4 5 6 H`

With what measurability are contributions tracked for existing systems to determine sustainability from initial projections and results?

`L 2 3 4 5 6 H`

With what certainty are encapsulated application and system processes reflective of current business drivers?

`L 2 3 4 5 6 H`

With what measurability is the organization forced to rework IT results with "downstream" systems to manipulate the output to meet the desired business result?

`L 2 3 4 5 6 H`

With what measurability are the business intelligence systems meeting corporate needs for:

A.   Customer intelligence and projections?

`L 2 3 4 5 6 H`

B.   Business operational forecasting?

`L 2 3 4 5 6 H`

C.   Competitive intelligence?

`L 2 3 4 5 6 H`

D.   Regulatory conformity?

`L 2 3 4 5 6 H`

E.   Risks analysis?   `L 2 3 4 5 6 H`

F.   Financial projections?   `L 2 3 4 5 6 H`

G.   Operational quality?   `L 2 3 4 5 6 H`

With what measurability are Internet efforts meeting required business needs regarding:

A.   Customer experience?   `L 2 3 4 5 6 H`

B.   Alliances and Joint Ventures?   `L 2 3 4 5 6 H`

C.   Contact centers?   `L 2 3 4 5 6 H`

D.   Web services?   `L 2 3 4 5 6 H`

E.   Blogging?   `L 2 3 4 5 6 H`

F.   Extranets?   `L 2 3 4 5 6 H`

G.   Extended processes?   `L 2 3 4 5 6 H`

H.   Sourcing?   `L 2 3 4 5 6 H`

I.   Globalization needs?   `L 2 3 4 5 6 H`

J.   Communications?   `L 2 3 4 5 6 H`

K.   Reporting/distribution?   `L 2 3 4 5 6 H`

L.   Replications?   `L 2 3 4 5 6 H`

M.   Collaborations?   `L 2 3 4 5 6 H`

With what quantifiability are total cost of ownership expenditures and investments (including supporting processes and procedures) in ERP systems resulting in:

A. Reduced product cycle time?   L 2 3 4 5 6 H

B. Faster time to market (from inception)?   L 2 3 4 5 6 H

C. Improved informational flow?   L 2 3 4 5 6 H

D. Increased quality?   L 2 3 4 5 6 H

E. Reduction in defects/scrap?   L 2 3 4 5 6 H

F. Improved organizational management   L 2 3 4 5 6 H
    (financial)?

G. Supply chain integration?   L 2 3 4 5 6 H

H. Elimination of duplicate efforts?   L 2 3 4 5 6 H

I. Faster response to competitive pressures?   L 2 3 4 5 6 H

J. Improved accuracy of results?   L 2 3 4 5 6 H

K. Increased customer satisfaction?   L 2 3 4 5 6 H

L. Substantial ROI?   L 2 3 4 5 6 H

M. Technical simplicity?   L 2 3 4 5 6 H

N. Reduced "inter-application" interfaces?   L 2 3 4 5 6 H

O. Data standardization?   L 2 3 4 5 6 H

P. Organizational consistency?   L 2 3 4 5 6 H

Q. Functional compartmentalization/reuse?   L 2 3 4 5 6 H

With what quantifiability are total cost of ownership   L 2 3 4 5 6 H
expenditures and investments (including supporting
processes and procedures) in CRM systems resulting in:

A. Improved customer communications? `L 2 3 4 5 6 H`

B. Customer insight and targeted marketing? `L 2 3 4 5 6 H`

C. Improved householding? `L 2 3 4 5 6 H`

D. Improved cross-selling? `L 2 3 4 5 6 H`

E. Reduced operating costs? `L 2 3 4 5 6 H`

F. Improved informational availability? `L 2 3 4 5 6 H`

G. Improved consistency of informational sourcing? `L 2 3 4 5 6 H`

H. Higher closing rate for new and existing customers? `L 2 3 4 5 6 H`

I. Improved channel effectiveness measures and comprehension? `L 2 3 4 5 6 H`

J. Detailed customer profiles? `L 2 3 4 5 6 H`

K. Increased customer loyalty? `L 2 3 4 5 6 H`

L. Higher yield for marketing and branding dollars? `L 2 3 4 5 6 H`

M. Improved customer personalization? `L 2 3 4 5 6 H`

N. Improved products the market wants? `L 2 3 4 5 6 H`

With what measurability are metrics tied to daily operational improvements at a shift level? `L 2 3 4 5 6 H`

With what measurability business continuance processes supported by business area requirements and analysis? `L 2 3 4 5 6 H`

With what measurability are business continuance cost justified?

`L|2|3|4|5|6|H`

With what measurability are business continuance efforts adjusted for operational, credit, market, and systemic risks?

`L|2|3|4|5|6|H`

With what measurability are reporting and distribution methods supportive of operational and planning objectives?

`L|2|3|4|5|6|H`

With what measurability are service level agreements used to allocate resources and funds for:

`L|2|3|4|5|6|H`

    A.   Availability?

`L|2|3|4|5|6|H`

    B.   Maintenance?

`L|2|3|4|5|6|H`

    C.   Costs?

`L|2|3|4|5|6|H`

    D.   Networks/Communications?

`L|2|3|4|5|6|H`

    E.   Recoverability?

`L|2|3|4|5|6|H`

    F.   Replications?

`L|2|3|4|5|6|H`

    G.   Outages?

`L|2|3|4|5|6|H`

With what measurability are definitive roles and responsibilities defined for all personnel?

`L|2|3|4|5|6|H`

With what measurability is security consistency integrated into the various applications?

`L|2|3|4|5|6|H`

With what measurability is the privacy and security of information protected from wrongful disclosure or destruction by:

`L|2|3|4|5|6|H`

A. Employees? `L|2|3|4|5|6|H`

B. Contractors? `L|2|3|4|5|6|H`

C. Partners? `L|2|3|4|5|6|H`

D. Service bureaus? `L|2|3|4|5|6|H`

E. Customers? `L|2|3|4|5|6|H`

With what measurability are informational assets recoverable in the event of a terrorist threat or natural disaster? `L|2|3|4|5|6|H`

With what measurability are employees protected against obsolescence due to changing skill requirements and globalization of corporate functions? `L|2|3|4|5|6|H`

With what quantification do the Service Level Agreements (SLA's) support the corporate level objectives? Business area objectives? `L|2|3|4|5|6|H`

With what measurability does the organization employ the adoption of enterprise architecture principles and operating philosophy? `L|2|3|4|5|6|H`

With what measurability does the organization utilize cross-department priority integration to manage IT resources and investments? `L|2|3|4|5|6|H`

With what quantifiability does IT use a priority ranking system to objectively assess business area needs and impact to operations? `L|2|3|4|5|6|H`

With what quantifiability are testing processes, methods, and techniques definitively integrated to SLA's and business area needs? `L|2|3|4|5|6|H`

With what measurability are purchases controlled by non-IT personnel where IT is only one of the recommenders of solutions?

`L 2 3 4 5 6 H`

With what measurability are definitive application and process techniques utilized for:

A. Rapid application development?

`L 2 3 4 5 6 H`

B. Application process extensions?

`L 2 3 4 5 6 H`

C. Extreme delivery?

`L 2 3 4 5 6 H`

D. Maintenance?

`L 2 3 4 5 6 H`

E. Production changes?

`L 2 3 4 5 6 H`

F. Reengineering?

`L 2 3 4 5 6 H`

G. Integration and interfacing?

`L 2 3 4 5 6 H`

H. Data management?

`L 2 3 4 5 6 H`

I. Testing?

`L 2 3 4 5 6 H`

J. Interfaces?

`L 2 3 4 5 6 H`

K. Security?

`L 2 3 4 5 6 H`

With what measurability does IT utilize consistent standards?

`L 2 3 4 5 6 H`

With what measurability are prototyping techniques used to prove concepts or implement systems?

`L 2 3 4 5 6 H`

With what applicability are new tools, techniques, and methods adopted as a result of business requirements?

`L 2 3 4 5 6 H`

With what measurability are standardized processes used for RFP/RFI's?   `L|2|3|4|5|6|H`

With what quantification are human resource systems used in:

    A.   Performance planning and appraisals?   `L|2|3|4|5|6|H`

    B.   Education and training?   `L|2|3|4|5|6|H`

    C.   Mentoring?   `L|2|3|4|5|6|H`

    D.   Separations?   `L|2|3|4|5|6|H`

    E.   Benefits and eligibility?   `L|2|3|4|5|6|H`

    F.   Personality testing?   `L|2|3|4|5|6|H`

    G.   Skills assessments?   `L|2|3|4|5|6|H`

    H.   Career counseling?   `L|2|3|4|5|6|H`

With what measurability are regulatory requirements addressed within existing system processes?   `L|2|3|4|5|6|H`

With what determinability can be assured when using informational to support due diligence or litigation efforts?   `L|2|3|4|5|6|H`

With what measurability is information irrefutable and recoverable to meet industry and regulatory requirements?   `L|2|3|4|5|6|H`

With what measurability do requirements typically meet or exceed business area needs when systems are promoted to production status?   `L|2|3|4|5|6|H`

With what measurability are technical costs outpacing business area benefits?

`L|2|3|4|5|6|H`

With what quantification is IT able to meet the changing needs of the business areas?

`L|2|3|4|5|6|H`

With what measurability are independent reviews used to confirm projected financial and quality benefits post-implementation?

`L|2|3|4|5|6|H`

With what measurability can data be used to audit IT system components to satisfy organizational, regulatory, and legal requirements?

`L|2|3|4|5|6|H`

With what measurability are operational control limits in place to effectively and efficiently monitor application, network, and system performance?

`L|2|3|4|5|6|H`

D. Systems and Operations

The use of the questions below must be adjusted and augmented with relevant industry and operational constraints. Therefore, not all questions will be applicable. Artifact sourcing should be obtained for all questions proposed.

With what quantifiability are systems, expansions, and supporting technology evaluated using total costs of ownership to derive benefits and expenses?

`L 2 3 4 5 6 H`

With what measurability are cross-industry practices and metrics ported to ascertain benefits, risks, and operational costs?

`L 2 3 4 5 6 H`

With what quantifiability are system backlogs managed?

`L 2 3 4 5 6 H`

With what measurability are systems and operational practices leveraged or removed before new ones are added?

`L 2 3 4 5 6 H`

With what quantifiability are success criteria utilized to evaluate programs and deliverables?

`L 2 3 4 5 6 H`

With what measurability are adequate roles and responsibilities for daily operations defined before system or process implementation?

`L 2 3 4 5 6 H`

With what measurability are data stores and warehouses leveraged to promote consistency of sourcing?

`L 2 3 4 5 6 H`

With what quantifiability are automation tools used to reduce costs, time to delivery and defects:

A.   Report generators?

`L 2 3 4 5 6 H`

B.   Data extractions?

`L 2 3 4 5 6 H`

C.   Systems management?

`L 2 3 4 5 6 H`

D.   Provisioning?

`L 2 3 4 5 6 H`

E.   Retention?

`L 2 3 4 5 6 H`

F.   Production lines?

`L 2 3 4 5 6 H`

G.   Test data?

`L 2 3 4 5 6 H`

H.   Testing harnesses?

`L 2 3 4 5 6 H`

I.   Contact center skill set routing?

`L 2 3 4 5 6 H`

J.   Industry automations?

`L 2 3 4 5 6 H`

With what quantifiability are systems and operational expenses properly allocated to the proper business units and product lines?

`L 2 3 4 5 6 H`

With what measurability are complete life-cycle costs accounted for in the unit costs of products or services (full allocations)?

`L 2 3 4 5 6 H`

With what quantifiability are productivity improvements attributed to direct system or operational process improvements?

`L 2 3 4 5 6 H`

With what determinability are system and operational improvements mapped to stated principles of operation to assure conformity?

`L 2 3 4 5 6 H`

With what measurability are the monitoring processes effective?

`L 2 3 4 5 6 H`

With what quantifiability are systems and operational processes directly contributing to the achievement of higher quality?

`L 2 3 4 5 6 H`

With what measurability are integration objectives communicated and tracked?

`L 2 3 4 5 6 H`

With what measurability do the systems and operations support the current organizational alignment and structures?

`L 2 3 4 5 6 H`

With what quantifiability are maintenance costs allocated to business areas or to product lines?

`L 2 3 4 5 6 H`

With what measurability are contract negotiations handled by trained personnel familiar with vendor interactions?

`L 2 3 4 5 6 H`

With what measurability do systems meet or exceed:

    A.   Customer satisfaction?

`L 2 3 4 5 6 H`

    B.   Required functionality?

`L 2 3 4 5 6 H`

    C.   Availability?

`L 2 3 4 5 6 H`

    D.   Operational directives?

`L 2 3 4 5 6 H`

    E.   Performance?

`L 2 3 4 5 6 H`

    F.   Volume/capacity?

`L 2 3 4 5 6 H`

    G.   Quality?

`L 2 3 4 5 6 H`

    H.   Informational content?

`L 2 3 4 5 6 H`

    I.   Process integration?

`L 2 3 4 5 6 H`

    J.   Interfaces?

`L 2 3 4 5 6 H`

    K.   Adaptability?

`L 2 3 4 5 6 H`

L.   Technology evolutions?

`L 2 3 4 5 6 H`

M.   Branding needs?

`L 2 3 4 5 6 H`

N.   Competitive differentiation?

`L 2 3 4 5 6 H`

With what determinability are system and operational improvements mapped to standards of operation to assure conformity?

`L 2 3 4 5 6 H`

With what measurability are definitive custodians defined for systems and operations?

`L 2 3 4 5 6 H`

With what measurability are components designed for reusability and cross-divisional leverage?

`L 2 3 4 5 6 H`

With what measurability are methods, tools, and techniques periodically reviewed for obsolesce and "decommissioning?"

`L 2 3 4 5 6 H`

With what quantifiability are systems and operations mapped to defined enterprise objectives?

`L 2 3 4 5 6 H`

With what measurability are centralized repositories used to actively managed system and operational functionality?

`L 2 3 4 5 6 H`

With what quantifiability are problems documented to forecast emerging trends?

`L 2 3 4 5 6 H`

With what quantifiability are fixes applied to systems or operational processes to ensure quality and delivery measures?

`L 2 3 4 5 6 H`

With what quantifiability are problem resolution changes tracked for quality and applicability post implementation?

`L 2 3 4 5 6 H`

With what quantifiability are system and operational processes measured for accuracy?

`L 2 3 4 5 6 H`

With what measurability are there definitive problem escalation procedures for critical systems?

`L 2 3 4 5 6 H`

With what measurability are all systems and operational processes classified with criticality and recoverability needs?

`L 2 3 4 5 6 H`

With what measurability are formalized reviews used to diagnosis trends, upcoming events, and change requests?

`L 2 3 4 5 6 H`

With what measurability are formalized approval processes used to promote systems and operations from test, user acceptance, system test, and production environments?

`L 2 3 4 5 6 H`

With what measurability are current systems and operations analyzed for conformity to projected requirements before introducing new ones?

`L 2 3 4 5 6 H`

With what measurability are technical considerations used in system and operational selection?

`L 2 3 4 5 6 H`

With what quantifiability are systems and operations used to ensure conformity to required internal controls and external reporting?

`L 2 3 4 5 6 H`

With what measurability are compliance and regulatory requirements considered when defining systems and operational changes/enhancements?

`L 2 3 4 5 6 H`

With what measurability security requirements incorporated into early stage designs?

`L 2 3 4 5 6 H`

With what measurability are audit standards enforced with all changes, enhancements, or introductions?

`L 2 3 4 5 6 H`

With what measurability are operational risks assessed with all introductions or changes?

`L 2 3 4 5 6 H`

With what measurability are audit reviews mandatory before the introduction of change?

`L 2 3 4 5 6 H`

With what measurability are there definitive data owners to govern access and dissemination of information?

`L 2 3 4 5 6 H`

With what quantifiability are changes grouped into releases or a batch of enhancements to avoid "one-off changes?"

`L 2 3 4 5 6 H`

With what quantifiability are "emergency" requirements allowed to by-pass standard operating procedures?

`L 2 3 4 5 6 H`

With what quantifiability are system and operational variation measured?

`L 2 3 4 5 6 H`

With what quantifiability are system and operational trends tracked and measured against control limits?

`L 2 3 4 5 6 H`

E. Programs, Projects, and Initiatives

The use of the questions below must be adjusted and augmented with relevant industry and operational constraints. Consequently, not all questions will be applicable. Artifact sourcing should be obtained for all questions proposed.

What is the total number of projects? _____

With what measurability are programs and projects complete with detailed plans?

`L 2 3 4 5 6 H`

With what measurability are all plans allocated with resources?

`L 2 3 4 5 6 H`

With what measurability are projects and programs completed with risk analysis plans?

`L 2 3 4 5 6 H`

With what measurability are critical assumptions documented?

`L 2 3 4 5 6 H`

With what measurability are deliverables and milestones defined for each plan?

`L 2 3 4 5 6 H`

With what quantifiability are estimates substantiated with prior heuristics?

`L 2 3 4 5 6 H`

With what measurability are project plans utilizing estimates to completion?

`L 2 3 4 5 6 H`

With what quantifiability are plans tracking actuals?

`L 2 3 4 5 6 H`

With what measurability are project or program defects identified and tracked?

`L 2 3 4 5 6 H`

With what measurability are interdependencies identified and tracked?

`L 2 3 4 5 6 H`

With what measurability do plans utilize experiential maps or suggested approaches?

`L 2 3 4 5 6 H`

With what quantifiability are outside services tracked, measured, and sourced per project or program?

`L 2 3 4 5 6 H`

With what measurability are program or project administration activities define and tracked:

A.   Issue management?

`L 2 3 4 5 6 H`

B.   Change management?

`L 2 3 4 5 6 H`

C.   Risk management?

`L 2 3 4 5 6 H`

D.   Project staffing?

`L 2 3 4 5 6 H`

E.   ETC?

`L 2 3 4 5 6 H`

F.   Milestones?

`L 2 3 4 5 6 H`

G.   Deliverables?

`L 2 3 4 5 6 H`

H.   Objectives?

`L 2 3 4 5 6 H`

I.   Budgets?

`L 2 3 4 5 6 H`

J.   Actuals?

`L 2 3 4 5 6 H`

K.   Time?

`L 2 3 4 5 6 H`

L.   Resources?

`L 2 3 4 5 6 H`

M.   Tasks?

`L 2 3 4 5 6 H`

N.   Red, Yellow, Green?

`L 2 3 4 5 6 H`

O. Contract documents? `L 2 3 4 5 6 H`

P. Employee/contractor reviews? `L 2 3 4 5 6 H`

Q. Stakeholder and sponsor reviews? `L 2 3 4 5 6 H`

R. Process changes? `L 2 3 4 5 6 H`

S. Communications and presentations? `L 2 3 4 5 6 H`

T. Testing and acceptance? `L 2 3 4 5 6 H`

U. Process and procedural adherence? `L 2 3 4 5 6 H`

V. Rework/duplication? `L 2 3 4 5 6 H`

With what quantifiability are tasks allocated to less than 40 hours? `L 2 3 4 5 6 H`

With what measurability are the proper skills sufficient to handle planned programs and projects? `L 2 3 4 5 6 H`

With what quantifiability are projects and programs overlapping? `L 2 3 4 5 6 H`

With what quantifiability are metrics indicative of plan progression? `L 2 3 4 5 6 H`

With what quantifiability are projects and programs successful when matched against:

A. Projected hours? `L 2 3 4 5 6 H`

B. Requirements? `L 2 3 4 5 6 H`

C. Deliverables? `L 2 3 4 5 6 H`

D. Rework?

`L 2 3 4 5 6 H`

E. Scope?

`L 2 3 4 5 6 H`

F. Customer/user acceptance?

`L 2 3 4 5 6 H`

G. Costs?

`L 2 3 4 5 6 H`

H. Financial returns?

`L 2 3 4 5 6 H`

I. Quality improvements?

`L 2 3 4 5 6 H`

J. Management expectations?

`L 2 3 4 5 6 H`

With what measurability are definitive roles and responsibilities defined?

`L 2 3 4 5 6 H`

With what measurability are owners defined for tasks and deliverables?

`L 2 3 4 5 6 H`

With what measurability are artifacts and documents catalogued and stored?

`L 2 3 4 5 6 H`

With what measurability are formalized reviews utilized to objectively review progress at set points within the programs and projects?

`L 2 3 4 5 6 H`

With what measurability are communications made available to:

A. Project staff?

`L 2 3 4 5 6 H`

B. Program managers?

`L 2 3 4 5 6 H`

C. Stakeholders?

`L 2 3 4 5 6 H`

D. Program sponsors?

`L 2 3 4 5 6 H`

E. Executive management? `L 2 3 4 5 6 H`

F. Board members and management
    committees? `L 2 3 4 5 6 H`

With what measurability are Intranet services used to
communicate progress and challenges? `L 2 3 4 5 6 H`

With what quantifiability are metrics summarized to
determine cause and effect relationships, projections,
and forecasts? `L 2 3 4 5 6 H`

With what measurability are formalized and proven
industry methods used to manage program and
project activities? `L 2 3 4 5 6 H`

With what measurability of certified project managers
used for daily management actions? `L 2 3 4 5 6 H`

With what quantifiability are statistical analysis
techniques used to assess progress and projections? `L 2 3 4 5 6 H`

With what measurability are standards employed to
manage, organize, control, and improve plans,
projects, and programs? `L 2 3 4 5 6 H`

F. Production Management

The use of the questions below must be adjusted and augmented with relevant industry and operational constraints. Therefore, not all questions will be applicable. Artifact sourcing should be obtained for all questions proposed.

With what measurability are resources actively managed for optimal performance?

`L|2|3|4|5|6|H`

With what measurability are services and resources managed for:

      A.   Workloads/capacity? `L|2|3|4|5|6|H`

      B.   Peak usage? `L|2|3|4|5|6|H`

      C.   Errors/scrap? `L|2|3|4|5|6|H`

      D.   Rework? `L|2|3|4|5|6|H`

      E.   SLA's? `L|2|3|4|5|6|H`

      F.   Quality? `L|2|3|4|5|6|H`

      G.   Setup? `L|2|3|4|5|6|H`

      H.   Delays? `L|2|3|4|5|6|H`

      I.   Severities? `L|2|3|4|5|6|H`

With what quantifiability are change requests introducing variability into the controlled/production processes?

`L|2|3|4|5|6|H`

With what measurability are business continuance efforts utilized to ensure continuous availability?

`L|2|3|4|5|6|H`

With what measurability are problem management
processes effective?

`L 2 3 4 5 6 H`

With what measurability is informational access
promoting improvements in:

    A.   Quality?

`L 2 3 4 5 6 H`

    B.   Capabilities?

`L 2 3 4 5 6 H`

    C.   Customer services?

`L 2 3 4 5 6 H`

    D.   Product delivery?

`L 2 3 4 5 6 H`

    E.   Collaborative services?

`L 2 3 4 5 6 H`

    F.   Performance indicators and measures?

`L 2 3 4 5 6 H`

    G.   Process synergies?

`L 2 3 4 5 6 H`

    H.   Process simplifications?

`L 2 3 4 5 6 H`

    I.   Consistency?

`L 2 3 4 5 6 H`

    J.   Forecasting?

`L 2 3 4 5 6 H`

    K.   Statistical analysis?

`L 2 3 4 5 6 H`

    L.   Change control?

`L 2 3 4 5 6 H`

    M.   Continuous availability?

`L 2 3 4 5 6 H`

With what measurability are procedural changes
analyzed for line or quality improvements?

`L 2 3 4 5 6 H`

With what measurability are production disruptions
tracked and analyzed for root-cause elements?

`L 2 3 4 5 6 H`

With what determinability are production disruptions escalated to problem owners for resolutions/actions?   `L 2 3 4 5 6 H`

With what determinability are human resources (HR) personnel actively managing:

    A.   Personnel separations?   `L 2 3 4 5 6 H`

    B.   Physical accessibility?   `L 2 3 4 5 6 H`

    C.   Performance management and appraisals?   `L 2 3 4 5 6 H`

    D.   Career developments?   `L 2 3 4 5 6 H`

    E.   Hiring standards/screening?   `L 2 3 4 5 6 H`

    F.   Positions, roles, and responsibilities?   `L 2 3 4 5 6 H`

    G.   Recruiting?   `L 2 3 4 5 6 H`

    H.   Background checks?   `L 2 3 4 5 6 H`

    I.   Disciplinary actions?   `L 2 3 4 5 6 H`

    J.   Goal setting?   `L 2 3 4 5 6 H`

    K.   Benefit administration?   `L 2 3 4 5 6 H`

    L.   Succession planning?   `L 2 3 4 5 6 H`

    M. HR processes?   `L 2 3 4 5 6 H`

    N. HR policies?   `L 2 3 4 5 6 H`

    O. HR procedures?   `L 2 3 4 5 6 H`

With what quantifiability are the HR functions outsourced?

`L 2 3 4 5 6 H`

With what measurability is HR utilizing a human resources information system (HRIS)?

`L 2 3 4 5 6 H`

With what measurability are triple constraints of schedule, time, and quality managed to peak efficiency?

`L 2 3 4 5 6 H`

With what measurability are personnel trained in the proper usage of:

`L 2 3 4 5 6 H`

    A.   Production facilities?

`L 2 3 4 5 6 H`

    B.   Contractors/outside services?

`L 2 3 4 5 6 H`

    C.   Machinery?

`L 2 3 4 5 6 H`

    D.   Testing environments?

`L 2 3 4 5 6 H`

    E.   Research materials?

`L 2 3 4 5 6 H`

    F.   Intellectual capital?

`L 2 3 4 5 6 H`

    G.   Software?

`L 2 3 4 5 6 H`

    H.   BPO?

`L 2 3 4 5 6 H`

    I.   Customer contact?

`L 2 3 4 5 6 H`

    J.   Effective communication?

`L 2 3 4 5 6 H`

    K.   Security?

`L 2 3 4 5 6 H`

    L.   Privacy?

`L 2 3 4 5 6 H`

M. Regulations?

`L 2 3 4 5 6 H`

N. Organizational policies?

`L 2 3 4 5 6 H`

O. Intranet/web usage?

`L 2 3 4 5 6 H`

With what measurability employee feedback incorporated into organizational actions and policies?

`L 2 3 4 5 6 H`

With what measurability does the organization employee 360 degree processes?

`L 2 3 4 5 6 H`

With what measurability are competitive demands incorporated into production schedules?

`L 2 3 4 5 6 H`

With what measurability are customer needs and volumes utilized to dynamically adjust:

`L 2 3 4 5 6 H`

A. Schedules?

`L 2 3 4 5 6 H`

B. Product mix?

`L 2 3 4 5 6 H`

C. Sourcing/supply chains?

`L 2 3 4 5 6 H`

D. Quality?

`L 2 3 4 5 6 H`

E. Channels?

`L 2 3 4 5 6 H`

F. Marketing messages?

`L 2 3 4 5 6 H`

G. Advertising?

`L 2 3 4 5 6 H`

H. Segmentation?

`L 2 3 4 5 6 H`

I. Interactions?

`L 2 3 4 5 6 H`

With what measurability are operational informational sources used to adjust production deliveries:

A. Reports?   `L 2 3 4 5 6 H`

B. Intranets?   `L 2 3 4 5 6 H`

C. Partner web sites? `L 2 3 4 5 6 H`

D. Competitive web sites? `L 2 3 4 5 6 H`

E. Industry publications and sites? `L 2 3 4 5 6 H`

F. Media reports?   `L 2 3 4 5 6 H`

G. Litigation?   `L 2 3 4 5 6 H`

H. Regulatory groups? `L 2 3 4 5 6 H`

I. World events?   `L 2 3 4 5 6 H`

J. Personnel/labor relations? `L 2 3 4 5 6 H`

K. Political changes? `L 2 3 4 5 6 H`

L. Business intelligence? `L 2 3 4 5 6 H`

M. Third party researchers? `L 2 3 4 5 6 H`

With what quantifiability are operational delivery's hindered/reduced by:

A. Network availability? `L 2 3 4 5 6 H`

B. Communication reliability? `L 2 3 4 5 6 H`

C. Cultural differences? `L 2 3 4 5 6 H`

D.   Time zones?   `L 2 3 4 5 6 H`

E.   Management focus?   `L 2 3 4 5 6 H`

F.   Organizational processes?   `L 2 3 4 5 6 H`

G.   Skill sets?   `L 2 3 4 5 6 H`

H.   Conflicting systems?   `L 2 3 4 5 6 H`

I.   Disparate informational sources?   `L 2 3 4 5 6 H`

J.   Outages?   `L 2 3 4 5 6 H`

K.   Language?   `L 2 3 4 5 6 H`

With what measurability are logs and journal entries
generated by systems used for:

A.   Problem determination?   `L 2 3 4 5 6 H`

B.   Trend analysis?   `L 2 3 4 5 6 H`

C.   Data mining?   `L 2 3 4 5 6 H`

D.   Security analysis?   `L 2 3 4 5 6 H`

E.   Due diligence?   `L 2 3 4 5 6 H`

With what quantifiability are business impacts
calculated for:

A.   Line outages?   `L 2 3 4 5 6 H`

B.   System outages?   `L 2 3 4 5 6 H`

C.   Facility loss?   `L 2 3 4 5 6 H`

D.   Critical personnel?   `L 2 3 4 5 6 H`

E.   Relationship loss?   `L 2 3 4 5 6 H`

F.   Information replication?   `L 2 3 4 5 6 H`

G.   Contact centers?   `L 2 3 4 5 6 H`

H.   Web servicing?   `L 2 3 4 5 6 H`

I.   Trade disputes?   `L 2 3 4 5 6 H`

J.   Border closings?   `L 2 3 4 5 6 H`

K.   Terrorist's actions?   `L 2 3 4 5 6 H`

L.   Strikers/walkouts?   `L 2 3 4 5 6 H`

M.   Anti-trust?   `L 2 3 4 5 6 H`

N.   Regulatory closings/actions?   `L 2 3 4 5 6 H`

O.   Fraud/criminal activities?   `L 2 3 4 5 6 H`

P.   Records loss/retainment?   `L 2 3 4 5 6 H`

Q.   Product/service liabilities?   `L 2 3 4 5 6 H`

With what determinability is there a comprehensive list of:

A.   Current inventory?   `L 2 3 4 5 6 H`

B.   Work in process?   `L 2 3 4 5 6 H`

C.   Skills by shift by location?   `L 2 3 4 5 6 H`

D. Procedural documentation?   `L 2 3 4 5 6 H`

E. Applications?   `L 2 3 4 5 6 H`

F. Technology?   `L 2 3 4 5 6 H`

G. Informational sources?   `L 2 3 4 5 6 H`

H. Informational uses?   `L 2 3 4 5 6 H`

I. SLA's?   `L 2 3 4 5 6 H`

J. Communication linkages and lines? `L 2 3 4 5 6 H`

K. Tools?   `L 2 3 4 5 6 H`

L. Methods?   `L 2 3 4 5 6 H`

M. Service models?   `L 2 3 4 5 6 H`

N. Metrics and measures?   `L 2 3 4 5 6 H`

O. Processes (including sub-processes)? `L 2 3 4 5 6 H`

P. Interfaces?   `L 2 3 4 5 6 H`

Q. Customers? By product? By value?   `L 2 3 4 5 6 H`

R. Vendors?   `L 2 3 4 5 6 H`

S. Outsourcers?   `L 2 3 4 5 6 H`

With what quantifiability are all the above actively managed to reduce:

A. Duplication?   `L 2 3 4 5 6 H`

B.   Maintenance?   `L 2 3 4 5 6 H`

C.   Costs?   `L 2 3 4 5 6 H`

D.   Complexity?   `L 2 3 4 5 6 H`

E.   Financial obligations?   `L 2 3 4 5 6 H`

F.   Risks?   `L 2 3 4 5 6 H`

G.   Outages?   `L 2 3 4 5 6 H`

H.   Overhead?   `L 2 3 4 5 6 H`

With what measurability are production operations continuously mapped to ensure obtainment of organizational:

A.   Metrics?   `L 2 3 4 5 6 H`

B.   Profits?   `L 2 3 4 5 6 H`

C.   Unit pricing?   `L 2 3 4 5 6 H`

D.   Market share and segmentation?   `L 2 3 4 5 6 H`

E.   Gross margins?   `L 2 3 4 5 6 H`

F.   Financial obligations?   `L 2 3 4 5 6 H`

G.   Objectives?   `L 2 3 4 5 6 H`

H.   Goals?   `L 2 3 4 5 6 H`

READING LIST

Business Process Management, Howard Smith and Peter Fingar, Meghan-Kiffer Press, 2004

Coaching, Mentoring, and Managing, William Hendricks, Career Press, 1996

GlobalWork, Mary O'Hara-Devereaux and Robert Johansen, Jossey-Bass Publishers, 1994

Managing Operation Risk, Douglas G. Hoffman, Wiley Finance, 2002

Making Enterprise Risk Management Pay Off, Thomas L. Barton, William G. Shenkir, and Paul L Walker, Prentice Hall, 2002

Successful Manager's Handbook, Personnel Decisions, Inc., 1992

INDEX

ENDNOTES

i Enterprise Resource Planning

ii Economics of the 1980's and 1990's were capital intensive. With the acceleration of Moore's Law, the costs to acquire and implement rapid advancements has placed the burden of results on personnel and their ability to take advantage of continuous technological change.

iii Member countries include Canada, France, Germany, Italy, Japan, United Kingdom, and the United States.

iv For a detailed analysis of principle centered leadership, see *IT Paradigm Shift*, by Don Tapscott and Art Caston, McGraw-Hill, 1993.

v As cited by ChemicalAlliance.org

vi See Abraham Maslow's Hierarchy of Needs.

vii All references to living or deceased personnel or organizations are purely coincidental.

viii Chief Information Officer

ix Abnormal Ends (Abends)

x Service Level Agreement

xi Chief Operating Officer

xii Return on Investment

xiii Internal Rate of Return

xiv Net Present Value

xv Is has been estimated that there are over 200 different certifications within information technology.

xvi Capability Maturity Model—see Carnegie Mellon Institute

xvii From experiential data and hands-on delivery spent over 20 years in the field.

xviii In the next five baseline subsections, it should be noted that the criteria presented will need to be adopted to meet your specific situation and organization. Not all criteria will apply and you may wish to add your own criteria to meet your particular requirements.

xix Global Positioning Systems

xx See Six Sigma methodology

xxi From experience, depending upon the technologies being utilized, this number can increase to over 25% for organization's employing unique or old technology. Some organizations have increased their risks by dropping support and maintenance agreements—they are too expensive to justify their payments.

xxii Quadrant lines omitted for readability

xxiii Business Process Management

xxiv Business Process Outsourcing

xxv Per Chemical Alliance.org, May 2004.

xxvi Edith Penrose was a US economist who in the 1950's created the foundation for applying "core competencies" to resource utilization.

xxvii From 2001 until 2004

xxviii Recent studies within the United States as cited by the Wall Street Journal have shown that over 11 million meetings take place every day within corporations. Respondents suggest that less than 15% of them serve any productive value.

xxix The selection of the proper expectation management formats has a great deal to do with the psychology and culture of the audience.

xxx Merger and Acquisition

xxxi Sources, Forbes, May 2004.

xxxii Compliance efforts should be considered the logical and physical implementation solutions used by corporations to meet the regulation.

xxxiii These systems would include defect prevention (*i.e.*, quality assurance) and detections (*i.e.*, quality control)

xxxiv ZYX Services is a fictitious company.

0-595-34246-9